From Fragmentation to Wholeness

RACE, ETHNICITY, AND COMMUNION

Neville Callam

Judson Press

From Fragmentation to Wholeness: Race, Ethnicity, and Communion
© 2017 by Judson Press, Valley Forge, PA 19482–0851
All rights reserved.

No part of this publication may be reproduced, stored in a retrieval system, or transmitted in any form or by any means, electronic, mechanical, photocopying, recording, or otherwise, without the prior permission of the copyright owner, except for brief quotations included in a review of the book.

Judson Press has made every effort to trace the ownership of all quotes. In the event of a question arising from the use of a quote, we regret any error made and will be pleased to make the necessary correction in future printings and editions of this book.

Scripture quotations are primarily from the New Revised Standard Version Bible, copyright © 1989 National Council of the Churches of Christ in the United States of America. Used by permission. All rights reserved worldwide.

Interior design by Scribe
Cover design by Wendy Ronga, Hampton Design Group

Library of Congress Cataloging-in-Publication data available upon request. Contact cip@judsonpress.com.

Printed in the U.S.A.

First printing, 2017

Dedicated to my wife,
Dulcie Allison

and our grandchildren,
Krista and Kari

CONTENTS

Acknowledgments   vii

Introduction   xi

1 Race: Manufacturing Inadmissible Diversity   1

2 Ethnicity: Establishing Borders of Exclusion   29

3 Communion: Celebrating Inclusive Community   51

4 Avoiding Fragmentation: Human Identity and Caribbean Theology   83

    Notes   107

ACKNOWLEDGMENTS

The four chapters of this book owe their origin to two main sources. The first is the Sam Sharpe Lectures presented in Manchester and Birmingham in the British Midlands in 2013. I am indebted to the sponsors of the Sam Sharpe Lectures for their cooperation that enabled the inclusion of a version of the original lecture entitled "Deconstructing the Notion of Race" as the first chapter of this book.

The Sam Sharpe Project developed in the wake of the November 2007 apology offered by the Council of the Baptist Union of Great Britain (BUGB) for their country's "share in and benefit from the transatlantic slave trade." It coincided with research on Sam Sharpe being developed at the Oxford Centre for Christianity and Culture, which led to an April 2010 initial conference on Sam Sharpe, sponsored jointly by the Centre and the BUGB, BMS World Mission, and the Jamaica Baptist Union.

Among the aims of the Sam Sharpe Project is the promotion of research into "the historical and theological legacy of Sam Sharpe and to reflect on the impact of this and other related stories for Baptist Christians in the 21st century."[1] I presented the second annual lectures, which were delivered on successive evenings at the Luther King House of the Northern Baptist Learning Centre in Manchester and at the BMS World Mission International Mission Centre in Birmingham, respectively. The Heart of England Baptist Association and Northern Baptist Learning Community joined the regular sponsors of the Sam Sharpe Project in sponsoring the 2013 Lectures.

My visit to the United Kingdom was expertly coordinated by Wale Hudson-Roberts, the racial justice coordinator for the BUGB. He was joined in graciously facilitating my stay in England by Gale Richards, project coordinator for the Heart of England Baptist Association and Rosemarie Davidson-Gotobed, event coordinator for the lectures. I acknowledge the kind hospitality received from Clare McBeath, Graham Sparkes, and the lecturers, staff, and students at the Northern Baptist Learning Centre in Manchester. I owe a similar debt of gratitude to the management and staff of the BMS Mission Centre and the Quaker House in Birmingham.

The second source for this book is the T. B. Maston Lectures on ethnicity and communion that were delivered in Abilene, Texas, in 2012, thanks to the cooperation of the T. B. Maston Foundation. The lectures were delivered at the Logsdon Seminary at the Hardin-Simmons University as part of the Lecture Series set up in honor of outstanding Baptist ethicist Thomas Buford Maston.

The T. B. Maston Foundation established the Lecture Series "to promote the legacy of T. B. Maston, a lifelong advocate for the deeper understanding and wider application of the life and ethical teaching of Jesus Christ."[2] Abridged versions of the lectures in their original form appeared in *Windows: Ministry Resources from the Logsdon School of Theology* 14.2 (Fall 2012). The original lectures appear in significantly expanded form as chapters two, three, and four of this book.

My stay in Abilene was made enjoyable particularly on account of the kind hospitality and helpfulness of my hosts, Bill and Leta Tillman. Both are influential leaders within the worldwide Baptist family. I acknowledge Bill's efficiency and care in overseeing the arrangements for my visit to Abilene. I also express gratitude for the hospitality of Hardin-Simmons University President Lanny Hall and his wife, Carol, and for the fellowship provided by Logsdon Seminary Professor Robert Sellers and his students.

I am grateful to the Baptist World Alliance (BWA) for giving me a seven-week sabbatical to enable me to make good progress in completing this book. I also acknowledge the valuable assistance received from my friends who offered helpful comments on earlier drafts of these chapters, and my friends on the staff of the BWA international office in Falls Church, Virginia, for the assistance they rendered.

This book is dedicated to my wife, Dulcie, who gave me much encouragement and support during the entire project. This was just another instance of her unwavering partnership with me that facilitates the service rendered to God during my entire ministry, including my years at the Baptist World Alliance. I am deeply indebted to her. Because our two grandchildren have brought us so much joy, the book is also dedicated to them. May they grow up in a world where increasingly people love and respect one another.

INTRODUCTION

Globalization can enhance integration or exacerbate division between nations. It can also engender the insecurity that influences social collectivities to assert their identity over against the identity of others. In this perspective, globalization tends to contribute to the breakdown of broad-based solidarities and the fragmentation of societies. The widespread use of language that serves to include some people and exclude others is supporting the divisiveness that globalization can inspire. This book investigates two terms—*race* and *ethnicity*—that have been employed in the program to divide humanity into separate, oppositional groups and contrasts them with a construct that imagines a world in which people embrace their mutual belonging.

Chapter 1 probes some aspects of the emergence of the ideology of race and examines some significant steps in the process of debunking the myth of biological constructions of race. While many churches and church organizations have denounced racism, which is predicated on ethnocratic pride in one's own racial grouping, the need for an ongoing deconstruction of the notion of race is advanced. Furthermore, it is suggested that, once the sin of racism is exposed and acknowledged, the church needs to take adequate steps to ensure that its witness in the name of Christ is not compromised by congregations that are still held hostage by the sin of racism.

The discussion of race is located in the context of a celebration of the values of Jamaican National Hero Samuel Sharpe, whose understanding of the meaning of human dignity is briefly characterized at the start of the chapter. While people continue to use the term *race* in a variety of ways, the strong likelihood of a popular use of the term to serve divisive ends needs to be acknowledged. Those who insist on continuing to attach biological criteria to their use of the language of race may need to be sanctioned.

The second chapter of this book deals with the subject of ethnicity. The author asserts that the language of ethnicity is often used to establish and maintain borders of inclusion and exclusion and suggests that Christians should examine their use of the term to ensure that it is not part of a toolkit of prejudice. The claim is made that the language of ethnicity can be helpful only if it is responsibly used in the service of constructing community solidarity within a multiethnic milieu.

If the use of the terms *race* and *ethnicity* is problematic for Christians who wish to eschew divisiveness in the way they understand and characterize humankind, then the author, in the third chapter of this book, argues that the Holy Communion (Lord's Supper or Eucharist) offers an opportunity for the Christian community to dramatize its inclusive and holistic view of humankind.

The chapter probes the extent to which the Holy Communion reinforces a Christian conviction concerning the unity of humankind. It begins by locating the Eucharist in the commensal traditions of both ancient Israel and the Greco-Roman world of the first few centuries of the Common Era. It identifies some aspects of the identity-forming nature of the Lord's Supper and also links the meal event with the mission of the church, drawing on insights from sources within the Christian tradition. It argues that the community-defining and solidarity-conferring dimensions of the worship event commit participants to a social ethic that embraces the unity of humankind and all creation.

The declarative and instrumental dimensions of the Lord's Supper can assist the church's quest for a proper response to the popular use of language that has the potential to divide people. Holy Communion can also inspire followers of Christ to offer a comprehensive witness against divisiveness. It reminds Christians that Jesus Christ crossed boundaries to open the way for Gentiles also to come under the reign of God. The Eucharist affirms the shared identity of those who enjoy fellowship in the body of Christ. It commits them to serve God's purpose of uniting humankind and all creation under the lordship of Christ. In the Lord's Supper Christians can commit themselves to the joy of true worldwide human solidarity.

The final chapter of this book provides one example of the danger of fragmentation that marks sincere efforts to use ethnicity to characterize how Caribbean people interpret the ways of God in their history.

Caribbean Theology developed out of the deep conviction that a "relevant theology" for the region should reflect the people's own experience of God. Instead of merely adopting an understanding of God emerging from the history of those who introduced Christianity to the region, Caribbean people are invited to investigate how God is at work among them and draw their own conclusions on the basis of the interplay between biblical teaching and their own reality. In developing this "relevant theology," Caribbean thinkers have related certain ways of understanding the incarnation to Caribbean ethnic identity and history as a source for their creative theological work. In this process, theologians have employed the language of ethnicity in a way that actually illustrates some of the dangers faced by those who couch their thoughts in a framework of ethnicity.

Acknowledging Caribbean Theology as a contextual theology, the author claims that a constructive appreciation of the ethnic profile of the population, discerned within an unobstructed view of the full context that Caribbean people share, is critical for the development of an authentic Caribbean theology of liberation. The delineation of a Caribbean

Theology profile is said to be fraught with difficulty because of the multiple identities of the people in whose voice such a theology speaks and also because of the fluidity of the identities these people negotiate from day to day.

Attention is drawn to the Caribbean context as a multi-religious one that is marked by a correlation between ethnicity and religious affiliation. Because the principle of the Incarnation is foundational to Caribbean Theology, it is argued that the claims associated with the Caribbean theological project must emerge from a full appreciation of the particularity of the context out of which that theology speaks. Only then can a constructive theology be truly reflective of the context in which it emerges.

Caribbean theologians who wish to be faithful as contextual theologians will also need to bear in mind the extent to which gendered constructs are embedded in local understandings of ethnicity. An appeal is made for these theologians to recognize the rich resource provided by the emerging tradition of critical reflection on the relation of gender and social development in the Caribbean. Insights from the available research findings can enable Caribbean theologians to respond meaningfully to the context in which, and for which, they claim to speak.

In 2009 the General Council of the Baptist World Alliance (BWA) established a Special Commission with responsibility "to discern an international, inter-cultural, inter-contextual hermeneutic" to support "the maintenance of the needed mutuality of and by diverse participants in the BWA movement."[1] In 2013, the Special Commission presented its report during the BWA General Council meeting. The Council adopted the Covenant on Intra-Baptist Relations proposed by the Commission. The Covenant takes the form of a set of principles and guidelines that are intended to assist those who attend BWA meetings to model the relationships and respectful dialogue that give expression to ideals that Baptist Christians share. There is a sense in which the Covenant on Intra-Baptist relations reflects the vision of the unity and harmony of humankind that this book embraces.

This book is based on the vision of a world in which people readily acknowledge the bonds of unity that hold them together in one universal, multicultural family. The members of this family agree that the images of each other that they develop and adopt can serve to reinforce this vision. Furthermore, the way they communicate with each other can also promote the idea of the unity of humankind. Unity in diversity is the hallmark of the vision of universal brotherhood and sisterhood whose full realization we await. A eucharistic hermeneutic may unlock the door to the rich possibility of living into this unity in the church today.

CHAPTER 1

Race
Manufacturing Inadmissible Diversity

From one ancestor [God] made all nations
to inhabit the whole earth.

Acts 17:26

There is no conceptual basis for race except racism.

Charles Hirschman[1]

Racial making has no basis in substance . . .
and the categories themselves are historical precipitates
of a five-hundred-year world epoch that we
must envision ending and that we must
struggle to hasten toward its end.

Roger Sanjeck[2]

The absolute equality of races, physical,
political and social is the founding stone of the world
and human achievement. [T]he voice of Science,
Religion, and practical Politics is one in denying the
God-appointed existence of super-races or of races
naturally and inevitably and eternally inferior.

Pan-African Congress, 1921[3]

> The black skin is not a badge of shame, but rather a glorious symbol of . . . greatness.
>
> *Marcus Mosiah Garvey*[4]

> [S]ilent racism—the racist thoughts, images and assumptions in the minds of white people, including those who by most accounts are "not racist"—is dangerous precisely because it is perceived as harmless.
>
> *Barbara Trepagnier*[5]

Is it time for the churches to take strong action to make it clear to those among its ranks that supporting racist practice and gladly harboring and supporting racists in its membership will no longer be tolerated?

In this chapter, starting with one of the national heroes of Jamaica, the author claims that the passion for human dignity and equality burns brightly in many human hearts. To offer lucid witness to this conviction, some have paid with their lives. Meanwhile, through the centuries, others have contributed to the creation of the groundwork to make racist ideology appear acceptable by associating the ideology with a veneer of professed scientific justification. Brief mention is made of some people whose role in this sad development is perhaps insufficiently canvassed. Yet much has been done to draw attention to the errors evident in scientific racism. Many international organizations have issued declarations to make clear where they stand on the matter of racism. This chapter identifies some of these developments.

Even without recourse to the history of the struggle against scientific racism, Christian thinkers have found, in the gospel and in the rich body of reflection on what God has revealed to the community of Christ-followers, enough to show the indefensibility of racism. Furthermore, significant examples can be found of instances in which Christian World Communions have taken a strong stand against churches that have stood up to offer strong support for institutional racism. After reflecting on some of these developments, the question arises concerning whether the time has come for organizations of churches to excommunicate those churches participating in their fellowship that not only support racism, but also provide a comfortable and hospitable home for proven and acknowledged racists. The foray into this painful scenario begins with the story of Samuel Sharpe.

Costly Witness to Human Dignity

The Right Excellent Samuel Sharpe, National Hero of Jamaica, was one of the principal collaborators in the project to secure liberation from enslavement for people residing in the Caribbean.[6] Born in Montego Bay, Jamaica, where he later worked as a "domestic slave,"[7] Sharpe's parents were among the millions of persons of African origin who were seized and forcibly removed from Africa with the intention of enslavement in the Caribbean and North and South America.[8] Indeed, the transatlantic trade in Africans has been described as

> the largest forced human migration in recorded history. The extent of the human suffering associated with this involuntary relocation of men, women and children may never be known. But their shipment—packed and stored beneath the deck of ships like commodities—constitutes one of the greatest horrors of modern times.[9]

Sharpe became a Christian and served as a deacon in the Baptist Church in Montego Bay. His formation in faith was facilitated mainly by the teaching of the missionaries sent from among the same European people who undertook to assault the dignity of enslaved Africans and to exploit their labor for pecuniary gain. However, he spent time reading the Bible for himself, and he came to recognize the fundamental error on which the sin of racism rests—the error that nourished the very roots of the system of slavery as it was practiced in the Caribbean. This is the odious belief that Sharpe, and those whose skin color looked like his, were not to be regarded as people who shared the same dignity and worth as those who exploited them. This belief is not unlike that found in the writings of Greek philosophers Aristotle and Euripides. As Aristotle put it: "From the hour of their birth, some men are marked out for subjection, others for rule. . . . It is clear that just as some are by nature free, so others are by nature slaves, and for these latter the condition of slavery is both beneficial and just."[10] Nor was it out of sync with the belief that was nurtured in Europe generally.

Sam Sharpe realized that the oppressive slaveholders believed that he, and others like him, lacked a rightful claim to the humanity the enslavers reserved for themselves. Resolute in his rejection of this belief, Sharpe was willing to offer up his life if his dignity would be continually disrespected and his humanity perpetually denied. "I would rather die on yonder gallows than live in slavery" are the immortal words he declared before his life was taken from him.[11]

Currently, we do not have access to any literary works by Sam Sharpe—the text of sermons he preached and Bible studies he delivered, for example. On account of this, we are forced to rely on secondary sources for an understanding of what Sharpe believed. Most of the available sources were compiled by members of the people who shared ethnic kinship with the oppressor class of slaveholders—which included dissenters among them.[12] Even when statements are attributed to Sharpe, these are reported by Europeans domiciled in Jamaica or on their own continent during the nineteenth century. The cumulative evidence from the available sources suggests the following generalized wording of four of Sharpe's convictions expressed in the language of the contemporary age.

First, all human beings are made by God, who invests in them dignity and rights that are inalienable and inviolable, including the right to be free.

Second, slavery is inconsistent with biblical teaching on human freedom because it represents the readiness to dehumanize persons and expresses fundamental disregard for the freedom of God. It is predicated on the idea that enslavers are entitled to exploit the enslaved for the enslavers' material advantage.[13] Sharpe's belief that slavery represents the commodification of the enslaved and their exploitation for the benefit of the enslavers is what lay at the very foundation of the "Baptist War."[14] Asked about the source for his idea that all people have a right to be free, Sharpe is reported to have identified this as the Bible.[15]

Third, since slavery represents a denial of human dignity, the enslaved have an obligation to take nonviolent action to secure their freedom. If, in the pursuit of their liberty through nonviolent protest, they encounter violence from those who oppress them, the enslaved are entitled to act in self-defense.

Fourth, it seems reasonable to assert that Sharpe understood that considerations of ethnicity were fundamental to the operation of the plantation economy in which black people were forced to serve the interests of white people. There is no avoiding the question of ethnicity and "race" when we are reflecting on the legacy of the Honorable Samuel Sharpe.

Sharpe knew that the practice of slavery in the Caribbean was undergirded by racist presumptions. According to Henry Bleby, Methodist missionary to Jamaica, Sharpe witnessed to having "learnt from his Bible that the whites had no more right to hold black people in slavery than the black people had to make the white people slaves; and for his own part, he would rather die than live in slavery."[16] Sharpe did not believe white people had any right to make merchandise of a human being. For him, slavery was a monstrous injustice.

Like Sharpe, many of the Africans who suffered the scourge of slavery felt the brunt of the violent disrespect for their dignity and humanity. They resisted the determined resolve of the estates to benefit from their labor without adequately compensating them. Eventually, many of the enslaved turned to violent protest as a last resort.

When Sharpe's forbears passed through "the door of no return," the captured Africans did not know what awaited them in the so-called New World. However, they would have had a premonition of it, when, piled up in a cellar such as the one at the place now called the Slave Castle in Ghana, they suffered brutal dehumanization while hearing the joyful sounds of Anglicans at worship in the room under which they were incarcerated.[17]

Transported to the Caribbean and sold to European businessmen by European traders, the enslaved lost every semblance of self-determination. They were now listed as part of the merchandise on the sugar estates on which they were forced to work.[18] In 1831 enslaved people in Western Jamaica responded to the denial of their humanity, the violation of their dignity, and the exploitation of their labor. They decided that, beginning immediately after Christmas Day, they would cease working until those who robbed them of the benefits they should derive from their toil were ready to offer them meaningful compensation. What they desired was two shillings and six pence per week, the amount paid to so-called "workhouse men."[19]

What Sharpe really desired was the purchase of freedom through the medium of a massive work stoppage. What eventuated, however, was the dusty brilliance of the nighttime sky as the enslaved put sugarcane plantations and buildings to the torch in the evening of December 27, 1831.[20] To use the words of Methodist missionary Henry Bleby, "It was not Sharpe's purpose to wade through blood to freedom, although he himself was prepared to die in pursuit of freedom."[21] Yet it was for that work stoppage and its subsequent rampage that he and several hundred others were executed.

Sam Sharpe scholar Delroy Reid-Salmon has stated that, after "excavating the layers of . . . mythology that engulf . . . the human subject in history," he was able to mine the treasure of Sharpe's affirmation of the equality of all human beings and the divine gift of freedom for everyone. Reid-Salmon offers a compelling interpretation of Sharpe's theological anthropology, which emerged in the crucible of the experience of chattel slavery.[22]

What Sharpe discerned from his reading of, and reflection on, Scripture led him to understand that any attempt to dehumanize people through their enslavement and the exploitation of their labor represented an unjustifiable and unwarranted assault on the dignity of the human race. Such was the valuation Sharpe put on slavery, that crime against humanity.

The Myth Undergirding Race Ideology

Yet slavery existed long before Europeans built a monument in its honor in the West Indies, and over the years it assumed many forms.[23] After the Germanic tribes captured what was an abandoned remote outpost of the Roman Empire, some of the people who lived in Britain were sold into slavery. However, it was the "civilised" Romans who introduced slavery to the "barbarians" of Western Europe, to borrow the description of Jamaican historian Richard Hart, who was familiar with the terms employed by the slavers of those days.[24] It is said that, at the start of the eleventh century, nearly 10 percent of the British population was enslaved.

Turning from Britain to the Iberian Peninsula, it is noteworthy that after Muslims from North Africa conquered the region from the Romans, they repelled their attackers and enslaved those who became prisoners of war. Over much of the period of their dominance, between 711 and 1492, the Muslims in Iberia enslaved both blacks and whites. As James Sweet has shown, they introduced "invidious distinctions" between black and white slaves, naming them differently as *'abd* and *mamluk* and treating them differently. White slaves served mainly as household helpers, and blacks were assigned the arduous tasks that needed to be done in the fields. Even free blacks were identified as *'abid* (plural of *'abd*).[25]

White Iberians living in the context of that prevailing Muslim attitude to blacks shared the same attitude themselves. And when the days of Iberian subjugation by the Moors came to an end, the Spanish and Portuguese powers, during the fourteenth century, looked for a zone over which to exert control and to expand their sphere of influence. They turned their attention to the south and west. By this time, however, they had already espoused notions of the inferiority of blacks that, in the eighteenth century, were refined by Europeans presenting themselves as scientists into an identifiable and clear racist ideology which predicated black inferiority on biological criteria.

The Iberian expansion project resulted in a form of slavery that reflects the deep depravity of the human mind. As Hart has said, "The ancient institution of slavery . . . was transplanted to the Americas where it was adapted . . . to serve a new commercial purpose. Its horrors were intensified a thousandfold."[26] Orlando Patterson's identification of slavery as "social death" describes very well the form of slavery that existed in the West Indies. The enslaved suffered a "perpetual condition of dishonor," being permanently and violently alienated from others and becoming socially dead.[27]

Slaveholders in the Caribbean were undoubtedly aware that those from whose dehumanization they profited were people whose ethnic origins were different from theirs. It is generally agreed, however, that when the British trade in slaves was at its height, racist thinking had not yet achieved its most heinous form. Over the centuries, the developing ideology of race was to acquire the mask of scientific foundation that was effective in its power to deceive its subscribers. Scientific racism mischaracterized the notion of race as a biological reality and bequeathed a legacy of white racism that many still struggle to overcome today.

Nor were the Iberians the only ones who helped construct the myth of blacks as inferior to whites. Other Europeans shared liberally in the manufacture of this most shameful ideological edifice that housed such persons as a bookkeeper from the New Yarmouth plantation in Vere, Jamaica, who, in 1823, informed the governor of Jamaica, "There are a race of beings that cannot bear prosperity. . . . It will be a lapse of ages before the Negro can even participate of the blessings of freedom; the very name of the African must cease to exist in their memories before their customs are obliterated."[28]

Strengthening the Foundations of Scientific Racism

Many Europeans helped lay the foundations for the rampant disrespect of human dignity that lies at the very heart of the idea of race as a biological category. Ivan Hannaford has claimed that "very little evidence [exists] of a conscious idea of race until after the Reformation."[29] Whether this is so or not, as James Sweet has observed, this is not to imply that racism did not exist until after the Reformation. Sweet has characterized the treatment of black Africans beginning in the Middle Ages as "racism without race."[30] This is in keeping with Orlando Patterson's observation that "the absence of an articulated doctrine of racial superiority does not necessarily imply behavioral tolerance in the relations between peoples of somatically different groups."[31]

The list of people who helped build the edifice of scientific racism is long, and some of the names included in it are likely to surprise those who are not familiar with some of their writings.

Among these are Swedish botanist Carl Linnaeus; German physician Johann Blumenbach, and French zoologist Jean Léopold Cuvier. Not to be omitted are four Britons—David Hume, Charles White, Thomas Carlyle, and Robert Knox.

Noted Scottish philosopher David Hume claimed that people who lived in the South "are inferior to the rest of the species and are incapable of higher attainment of the human mind."[32] Although he did not support slavery which, according to his utilitarian calculus, was not advantageous to the overall happiness of humankind, Hume had little respect for blacks, whom he described in the following words: "You may obtain anything of the NEGROES by offering them strong drink; and may easily prevail upon them to sell, not only their children, but their wives and mistresses, for a case of brandy."[33]

In a footnote appearing in one of his works, Hume said: "There never was a civilized nation of any complexion than white," and he opined that "in Jamaica, indeed, they talk of one Negro as a man of parts and learning, but 'tis likely he is admired for very slender accomplishments like a parrot who speaks a few words plainly."[34] Hume attempted damage control when, criticized for this claim, he revised the footnote containing this claim for later publication of his work. He stated instead that he was "apt to suspect the Negroes to be naturally inferior to the whites" and that "there scarcely ever was a civilized nation of that [black] complexion, nor even any individual eminent either in action or speculation."[35]

England produced Charles White, the physician who founded the Manchester Royal Infirmary, and who, in 1799, described white people as "the most beautiful of the human race." Claiming that whites were the "most removed from brute creation," White claimed that "no one will doubt [the] superiority" of white people.[36]

Over the years, many other well-known figures helped promote the idea of the superiority of white people over blacks. In 1849, in an address to those he deemed his "philanthropic friends," Scottish historian Thomas Carlyle[37] spelled out what he called his "painful duty" to remind them of the estate of blacks who, in his opinion, were created with the endowments to make them fit to serve their white European masters. Of the blacks in the West Indies, he said:

> [An idle black person has] the right . . . to be *compelled* to work as he was fit, and to *do* the Maker's will, who had constructed him with such and such prefigurations of capability. And I incessantly pray Heaven, all men, the whitest alike, and the blackest, the richest and the poorest, in other regions of the world, had attained precisely the same right, the divine right of being compelled (if "permitted" will not answer) to do what work they are appointed for, and not to go idle another minute, in a life so short!

In 1850 Scottish anatomist Robert Knox[38] argued passionately for the superiority of whites over others, especially blacks:

> With me, race, or hereditary descent, is everything; it stamps the man. . . . The races of men . . . differ from each other widely—most widely.[39]
>
> [T]he races of men are not the result of accident; they are not convertible into each other by any contrivance whatsoever. The eternal laws of nature must prevail.[40]
>
> Look all over the globe, it is always the same; the dark races stand still, the fair progress.[41]
>
> I feel disposed to think that there must be a physical, and consequently, a psychological inferiority in the dark races generally . . . [owing to] perhaps specific characters in the quality of the brain itself.[42]

Knox concluded that the "black races" cannot become civilized. "Their future history must resemble the past. The Saxon race will never tolerate them."[43] Black people are different from white people "in everything as much as in colour."[44] He believed that "the races of men when carefully examined will be found to show remarkable *organic* differences."[45]

Whatever may be the disparate estimates of the contribution of each of the persons already mentioned, hardly is there any doubt concerning the significance of Swedish scientist Carl Linnaeus' contribution to the attempt to predicate racism on a scientific foundation. It was no less a person than Swiss philosopher Jean Jacques Rousseau, who sent the following message to Linnaeus: "Tell him I know no greater man on earth."[46] Linnaeus had developed a taxonomy[47] that included categories of species with white Europeans at the top and black Africans at the bottom of the human species. In this taxonomy, which perhaps still commands its band of supporters today, Linnaeus adopted a fourfold categorization of people as follows:

- *Homo Europaeus*, having white skin and identified as gentle and governed by laws;
- *Homo Americanus*, with red skin and said to be choleric (irritable and easily angered) and governed by customs;
- *Homo Asiaticus*, with yellow skin and described as haughty and governed by opinion; and
- *Homo Afer*, with black skin and characterized as indolent and governed by caprice.[48]

What Linnaeus attempted was a scientific taxonomy in which phenotype or skin color and alleged behavioral characteristics were purported to be related biologically. His theory provided what he considered a scientific foundation for a classification of people. It provided the bedrock, deemed respectable by the unsuspecting, on which the edifice of the evil system of scientific racism was firmly erected.

With the passage of time, the study of "race" that Linnaeus started mushroomed. In 1795, in the third edition of his work, *On the Natural Varieties of Mankind*,[49] German physician and anthropologist Johann Blumenbach identified five varieties of humankind: the Caucasian or white race; the Mongolian or yellow race; the Malayan or brown race; the Ethiopian or black race; and the American or red race. At first Blumenbach held that "the white color holds the first place," with people of other skin color being mere degenerates of the original.[50] Eventually he attributed skin color to geography and diet and concluded that Africans belong to the human family and are not inferior to the other so-called races. In the end and happily, Blumenbach did not assign immutability to the classification system he had developed.[51]

In the nineteenth century, French zoologist Jean Léopold Cuvier, sometimes referred to as Georges Cuvier, reduced Blumenbach's race classification from five to three: Caucasian, comprising white people, with Adam and Eve as their progenitor in what Cuvier claimed was the original race; Mongolian—yellow people; and Ethiopians—black people. Blacks, he said, were "the most degraded of human races, whose form approaches that of the beast and whose intelligence is nowhere great enough to arrive at regular government."[52]

It took many years for the scientific community to effectively expose the pseudo-science that was used to justify white people demeaning and subjugating black people. With increasing awareness of the fiction of biological notions of race, many people were able to support the march toward the emancipation of slavery and the concomitant humanization of slaveholders.

Debunking the Myth of Biological Race

In the post-Enlightenment period, during which the idea of race achieved full expression as an ideology, many people subscribed to the opinion that there are "immutable major divisions of humankind, each with biologically transmitted characteristics."[53] Each "race" was deemed "a homogeneous group of individuals biologically or linguistically similar to one another and systematically distinguishable" from other so-called races.[54] Over time, prevailing opinion on race became markedly different from what it was in the seventeenth and eighteenth centuries.

In the aftermath of World War I, a Peace Conference convened in Paris, France, was expected to herald a new world order rising from the ash heap created by the war. Some participants hoped the conference would affirm the principle of equality among people deemed to belong to different racial groupings. However, the contributions of significant white delegates underlined the firm resolve of certain nations, especially Britain, the United States, South Africa, and Australia, to maintain the principle of racial inequality.

British representative Harold Nicholson balked at any suggestion that "implied the equality of the yellow man with the white man," not to mention what he termed "the terrific theory of the equality of the white man with the black."[55] British Prime Minister David Lloyd George—who is reputed to have been a Baptist[56]—made an impassioned plea for France not to train what he termed "big nigger armies."[57] In the end, it was United States President Woodrow Wilson who managed to ensure the derailment of the intention of the majority on the League of Nations Commission to affirm "the principle of equality of nations and just treatment of nationals."[58]

When, in 1948, the United Nations (UN) issued the International Declaration of Human Rights, the groundwork was laid for the undermining of the assumptions informing the ideology of race and thus the justification of racism. Two years later the United Nations Educational, Scientific and Cultural Organization (UNESCO) issued a *Statement on Race*,[59] declaring:

> Scientists have reached general agreement in recognizing that mankind is one; that all men belong to the same species, *homo sapiens*. §1
>
> For all practical social purposes, "race" is not so much a biological phenomenon as a social myth . . . [that] has created an enormous amount of social damage. §14[60]

If all human beings belong to one race, then it would follow that racism is inconsistent with respect for human rights. Not surprisingly, in 1963 the UN General Assembly approved a resolution affirming the Declaration on the Elimination of All Forms of Racial Discrimination. According to that declaration,

"Any doctrine of racial differentiation or superiority is scientifically false, morally condemnable, socially unjust and dangerous, and . . . there is no justification for racial discrimination either in theory or in practice."[61]

In 1965 the UN adopted and opened for signature and ratification the International Convention on the Elimination of All Forms of Racial Discrimination. A year later the UN designated March 21 as the International Day for the Elimination of Racial Discrimination. By 1967 UNESCO gave fuller expression to its understanding of race in a *Statement on Race and Racial Prejudice*.[62] A UNESCO committee of experts from seventeen countries declared:

> All men living today belong to the same species and descend from the same stock. §3a
>
> Current biological knowledge does not permit us to impute cultural achievements to differences in genetic potential. §3c
>
> Racism falsely claims that there is a scientific basis for arranging groups hierarchically in terms of psychological and cultural characteristics that are immutable and innate. §5

During the 1970s the UN General Assembly adopted the International Convention on the Suppression and Punishment of the Crime of Apartheid. It also declared 1973–1982 as the Decade for Action to Combat Racism and Racial Discrimination. The hope was that the period would be used for concrete action to eliminate the evils it identified. Needless to say, at the end of the decade little had changed in attitudes to race. Not surprisingly therefore, the UN subsequently found it necessary to declare a second Decade for Action to Combat Racism and Racial Discrimination—1983–1992, and then later a third, 1994–2003. During the third decade, certain groups within the scientific community made significant decisions to register their rejection of the ideology of race. Take, for example, the "Statement on Race" issued in 1998 by the American Anthropological Association. It explicitly states that:

> With the vast expansion of scientific knowledge . . . it has become clear that human populations are not unambiguous, clearly demarcated, biologically distinct groups. . . . Evidence from the analysis of genetics . . . indicates that most physical variation, about 94%, lies *within* so-called racial groups. Conventional geographic "racial" groupings differ from one another only in about 6% of their genes. This means that there is greater variation within "racial" groups than between them. . . . Physical variations in the human species have no meaning except the social ones that humans put on them. . . . "[R]ace" was a mode of classification linked specifically to peoples in the colonial situation. It subsumed a growing ideology of inequality devised to rationalize European attitudes and treatment of the conquered and enslaved peoples. . . . Ultimately "race" as an ideology about human difference was subsequently spread to other areas of the world. It became a strategy for dividing, ranking, and controlling colonized people used by colonial powers everywhere. . . . Given what we know about the capacity of normal humans to achieve and function within any culture, we conclude that present-day inequalities between so-called "racial" groups are not consequences of their biological inheritance but products of historical and contemporary social, economic, educational, and political circumstances.[63]

Based on unequivocal affirmations on race, the UN convened World Conferences to Combat Racism and Racial Discrimination. The first meeting took place in Geneva, Switzerland, in 1978, and the second in Durban, South Africa, in 2001. The Conference Statement produced by the Second World Conference against Racism, Racial Discrimination, Xenophobia and Related Intolerance reaffirmed principles earlier adumbrated by the UN. Notably, it recognized, "with grave concern that, despite the efforts of the international community, the principal objectives of the three Decades to Combat Racism and Racial Discrimination [had] not been attained and that countless human beings [continued] to the present day to be victims of racism, racial discrimination, xenophobia and related intolerance."⁶⁴ The Conference affirmed:

> [R]acism, racial discrimination, xenophobia and related intolerance, where they amount to racism and racial discrimination, constitute serious violations of, and obstacles to, the full enjoyment of all human rights and deny the self-evident truth that all human beings are born free and equal in dignity and rights . . . and are among the root causes of many internal and international conflicts . . . and the consequent forced displacement of populations.

Firmly "rejecting any doctrine of racial superiority, along with theories that attempt to determine the existence of so-called distinct human races," and reaffirming that "all peoples and individuals constitute one human family, rich in diversity," the Conference emphasized the need for "a global fight against racism, racial discrimination, xenophobia and related intolerance and all their abhorrent and evolving forms and manifestations" and called this "a matter of priority for the international community." The Conference also proposed a program of action designed to address the scourge of racism that continues to be evident today.

Since that Conference, further action has been taken in the scientific community to help consolidate the gains contingent upon the rejection of the alleged scientific foundation for the idea of a firm link between biology and "race."

In 2011 the International Union of Anthropological and Ethnological Sciences issued its own *Statement on Race and Racism*,⁶⁵ which declared:

> All humans living today belong to a single species, *Homo sapiens*, and share a common descent. All living human populations have evolved from one common ancestral group over the same period of time. §1
>
> For centuries, scholars have sought to comprehend patterns in nature by classifying living things. Attempts to classify human populations in this manner have been wholly misplaced . . . [H]umanity cannot be

classified into discreet geographical categories on the basis of biological differences. §5

There is no necessary concordance between biological characteristics and culturally defined groups. §10

Eloise Meneses, in her succinct summary of the basis of the rejection of the pseudoscience of race, presents three postulates:[66] First, a much greater variation marks other species than the very narrow gene pool human beings form. Second, most of the physical variations discernible among human beings are not characteristic of any specific group of people, but are spread throughout the entire human population. Third, all human beings are genetically related, and the slight variations between populations do not indicate race lines. As she explains: "There are no pure stocks among us; nor have there ever been in the past. . . . Put simply, there is no such thing, nor has there ever been in the biological world [such a thing] as race."[67] Meneses adds a critically important observation:

> The social construction of race does not make the biological existence of race a fact. The myth of biological race needs to be debunked in our own minds and in others'. As long as people believe that humanity is "naturally" divided into biological races, they will give a significance and a finality to ethnic groups that is not warranted.[68]

The alleged scientific basis for the notion of biological race has been rejected by most scientists, sociologists, and anthropologists, many of whom have helped clarify that race is a socially constructed identity. It does not correspond to any set of biological features which were once used as a basis for dividing humankind into different "racial" groupings. It is now generally agreed that biologically there is only one race—the human race. And the "races" some people have reified are social constructs that are not based on biology, but represent a strategy of dominant ethnic groups that wish to assert their "superiority" over others. The existence of so-called "races" has been debunked.

When the World Council of Churches (WCC) deliberated on the subject of race and racism at its Fourth Assembly in 1968, it did so in the context of the discussion on race that was taking place in the international community. The WCC identified the features of racism in the following terms:

- ethnocentric pride in one's own racial group
- preference for the [alleged] distinguishing characteristics of that group
- belief that these group characteristics are fundamentally biological in nature and are transmitted to succeeding generations
- strong negative feelings toward other groups who do not share the defining characteristics of their group
- efforts to discriminate against and exclude the outgroup from full participation in the life of the community[69]

Unfortunately, all the clarifying statements about race and the exposure of the baseless claims about the link between biology and "race" have not succeeded in eliminating the problem of racism. Racism continues to be ubiquitous.

Looking toward the Future

Racism is a problem as much within the church community as outside it, and over and over again, the Baptist World Alliance (BWA) has taken a stand against it. BWA has issued a steady stream of statements against racism—none of the statements treating the fundamental question of the myth of biologically based notions of race.[70] BWA has reflected awareness of the church's urgent need to take action, grounded in its faith, to revolutionize the way it deals with the subject of race. What the church needs to do is to deconstruct the notion of race and register progress on the road to people truly loving others following the pattern Jesus taught and exemplified. Animated by a renewed commitment, the church can take effective action not only to correct prevailing understandings of racism within its rank but also discourage and discountenance the practice of racism by its members.

Churches need to urge their members to recognize that the association of biology and race constitutes the very foundation of the problem of race and racist ideology. They need to explain that this ideology is a human creation designed both to make perceived inequality between people appear to be inborn and to reinforce the belief that it is part of the taken-for-granted landscape of human life. If Christians today are to come to terms with the serious problem reflected in popular understandings of race, three steps need to be taken.

First, the church needs to expose a fundamental misunderstanding of the divine nature that undergirds the ideology of race. This is the error of segregating human freedom from its foundation and grounding in divine freedom. God, by whose own volition the world was created and in whose providence human beings are entrusted with the stewardship of creation, has endowed humankind with the gift of freedom. In sovereign freedom, God bestows liberty on human beings whom God has made, and God wants this liberty to be respected. The denial of the freedom that rightly belongs to each human being represents a rejection of the divine design for creation. As Noel Erskine has said, "Whenever the church fails to make the connection between divine freedom and human freedom, it supports and gives its blessings to vicious structures of oppression in our world."[71]

Commenting on the biblical narrative of creation, Dwight Hopkins has stated that "God breathed the Spirit of liberation, the Spirit to be free, into the very act of creation itself . . . (Gen 2:7)."[72] The freedom each human being receives is "the freedom inherent in God's own self."[73] The gift of freedom entails freedom

> to enjoy all of God's work without . . . external negative restrains of any kind. In sum, human beings were brought into existence to

be in equal relationship at each stage of their interactions. . . . God implanted liberation in the created human beings . . . [so that] this liberation may be enacted on the everyday and ordinary levels of existence.[74]

To deny human beings the capacity to exercise their liberty freely is to fly in the face of the Creator who is the giver of freedom. The church needs to rediscover and consistently affirm the link between divine freedom and human freedom and place this link at the center of its discourse on what it means to be a part of God's creation.

Second, Christians may need to intentionally reengage the Christocentric faith that highly values what God has accomplished for the salvation of the world through the sacrifice of Christ. This is an important requirement if Christians are to come to terms with and develop the resolve to work consistently to overcome the serious problem that inheres in a biological understanding of race.

Human beings ought not to allow their God-given freedom to be contaminated by distorted understandings, false pride, or the pursuit of power. When, through his life, death, and resurrection, Jesus Christ secures victory over sin, God swings the door wide open for the renewal and reinvigoration of what it means to be truly human. God enables people to see the self and the other as equally valid expressions of God's mysterious action in creation and redemption. Then, the way of the follower of Christ will reflect the grammar of that mutual respect and *agape* love that are perfectly inhospitable to any claim of inherent superiority of one person over another. Our Christocentric faith reflects our Lord's action in breaking down the walls that separate people from one another, releasing them for the wholesome enjoyment of *Ubuntu*, the principle of human solidarity and reciprocity.

In a 1997 White Paper on Welfare, the South African government expressed its understanding of *Ubuntu* in the following terms:

> [*Ubuntu* is] the principle of caring for each other's well-being . . . and a spirit of mutual support. . . . Each individual's humanity is ideally expressed through his or her relationship with others and theirs in turn through a recognition of the individual's humanity. Ubuntu means that people are people through other people. It also acknowledges both the rights and the responsibilities of every citizen in promoting individual and societal well-being.[75]

In the perspective of *Ubuntu*, a trinitarian Christocentric faith will not accommodate the negative images of others, and of otherness, that are created and utilized as identity markers to galvanize feelings of superiority over others.[76] Instead, people will assign to each and every person the primary identity of a human being and, with fellow Christians, a shared identity in Jesus Christ.

With the passage of time, people have displayed their incredible capacity for inventing identities for groups of people belonging to other cultures. They have assigned them such names as barbarians, savages, infidels, pagans, heathen, unenlightened, children, aboriginals, or natives. These identities help people entrench and maintain dominance over others and find grounding for their patronizing gestures toward them. With a truly Christocentric faith, Christians are capable of imagining how human diversity finds a safe home within the one mystical body of Christ where no one is demeaned or disrespected and all who confess Christ are welcome at the Table of Life.[77]

It is supremely in Jesus Christ, who is the icon of the invisible God, that one sees the full manifestation of the freedom bequeathed to all Christians. This freedom is marked by self-emptying love—the love that reaches out for the sake of the beloved rather than as part of a utilitarian game pursued in search of personal honor, glory, or "success." The selfless love that can be part and parcel of people's affirmative response to Christ provides an avenue through which to secure the liberation of creation. Christocentric faith opens up space for covenantal relationships geared toward the edification of all and the enhancement of the welfare of the whole community.

Christians also need to rediscover and constantly reaffirm the pneumatological dimensions of faithful Christian living. Only then will the church be ready to appropriate the power to discern the ways in which sin is at work in the structures and arrangements that serve the cause of human domination.

The Holy Spirit opens our understanding to our vocational obligation to live with the symphony of existential relatedness with God and with other human beings within the community of the whole creation. Enlivened by the Holy Spirit, human beings discern the contours of what Barbara Trepagnier calls "silent racism"—the unspoken racist thoughts and unacknowledged racist assumptions that inform the attitudes many people display, and that contribute to the stereotypes we invent and the institutions we develop.[78]

The Spirit alone can cleanse the human mind, enabling human beings to understand ways in which many of them are beneficiaries of institutional racism that, whether they like it or not, makes them complicit in the sin from whose perpetration they continue to reap privileges and benefits. It is the Holy Spirit who will help followers of Christ detect what Charles Mills calls the "racial contract" that is presupposed by the social contractarianism that informs, and is implicit in, much of our contemporary political discourse and arrangements.[79]

Jürgen Moltmann caught a glimpse of the freedom the Holy Spirit brings when he referred to the church as "a fellowship of the free." The church, he says, is "an order of freedom" in which "people are freed from the oppression which separates them from others" and are liberated "for free fellowship with one another."[80] In this community the negative identities we construct for ourselves and others cannot stand in the light of the new reality God calls the church to unveil before the world.

The Holy Spirit enables every Christian to see that each person is created and loved by God and enjoys the heritage of the freedom given in Christ. As a community living under the reign of Christ, the church recognizes that, under this rule, the pernicious forces of this world have been undermined and the cruel powers dethroned. As a result of this, the church becomes, in the words of Moltmann, "the fellowship of Christ through faith and hope, discipleship and new fellowship," manifesting what it means to be freed by Christ and to live in the power of the Holy Spirit. A rediscovery of both the place of the Holy Spirit in the life of Christ-followers and the process of sanctification in the lives of the faithful is of vital importance to living out the loving relations that should characterize the Christian community.

If the church takes the steps identified above, Christians will become more capable of discerning the radical importance and significance of the creation of humankind in the image of God. They will recognize that the living out of the faith on the bedrock of an informed and defensible theological anthropology is the *sine qua non* of genuine Christian discipleship. By reading the Scriptures in the key of this rounded theological anthropology that "interrogates what people are created and called to be and to do,"[81] several challenges may be met and overcome.

First, one will be disposed to reject the heretical claims regarding enslavement of black people as just payment for the sin of Ham.[82] Second, one's approach will thoroughly undermine the claims of those who ascribe culpability to the Creator for the racist ideology that denies the equal dignity of all human beings created by the one God. Racists accomplish this by claiming that the instinct to regard others as inferior to oneself is consistent with divine providence.[83] This applies especially to white people who are inheritors of what Caroline Redfearn describes as "the theological racism that humanity was originally White."[84] Third, those who read Scripture through the lens of a mature theological anthropology will be led to identify with the thoroughgoing critique of social injustice in the tradition of the great prophets of ancient Israel and to embrace, with joyful abandon, Jesus' ethic of radical love of neighbor.

As J. Kameron Carter has pointed out, Christ-followers need to engage the creative theological imagination that makes possible a reading of Scripture "against, rather than within, the social order."[85] When this way of reading Scripture is pursued, the sharp edges of the dagger of racism will be rendered useless against the impenetrable rock of informed faith. The same theological anthropology that grounds the equality of women and men and inspires commitment to a just social order undergirds the conviction that the combined effects of racial and gender discrimination hinder the advancement of women and diminish the likelihood of their equality with men being acknowledged.[86]

In light of all that has been said above, could it be that a *status confessionis* has arrived in relation to any church congregation that denies that racism is sin, refuses to affirm that those Christians who practice and defend it are compromising their standing in Christ, and refrains from taking concrete and decisive action to root out racism from its life? By not participating in the struggle to overcome racism—an "assault on human dignity and Christian conscience"[87]—should one not conclude that a congregation has turned its back on the truth that is in Christ and has become a pseudo-church?

Taking a Stand

It was in his profound disappointment with the church under Nazi Germany, and more specifically with the watering down of the first draft of the Bethel Confession,[88] that Dietrich Bonhoeffer called attention to *status confessionis*. This idea refers to the existence of a situation that threatens to destroy the integrity of the church's confession of faith. Such a situation demands a restatement of the faith that inevitably includes a distinction between "true" and "false" church.[89]

By invoking the *status confessionis*, the church declares that Christians and churches defending a position that is profoundly unchristian are guilty of heresy.[90] This means that the ecclesial proponents and defenders of seriously flawed sociopolitical and ethical beliefs are seen to be disqualifying themselves from participation in the wider family of Christ's church. They have ceased to be, and can no longer be regarded as, churches in the true sense because they have forsaken, and are living in corporate betrayal of, the true Gospel and its just demands.[91]

At least two Christian World Communions have applied the concept of *status confessionis* in their relation to apartheid. The Lutheran World Federation (LWF) took this action in 1977,[92] and the World Alliance (now World Communion) of Reformed Churches (WCRC) did the same in 1982.[93] The attitude of certain churches to apartheid was what precipitated this outcome. Through their support and defense of institutional racism, the Dutch Reformed Church in South Africa, for example, jeopardized the integrity of the Gospel and rejected solidarity with the body of Christ.[94]

The drastic action of declaring that a *status confessionis* has arrived in relation to certain churches is needed in our times. National ecclesial organizations need to declare a *status confessionis* in relation to their member churches—that is, their member congregations—that endorse racist ideology and encourage racist practice. This action is necessary because, in spite of the time and effort churches have committed to identifying and advocating against the sin of racism, the problem of racism remains intractable. The responsiveness of sections of the church community to the ubiquity of racism has been sluggish. Ecclesial inaction in the face of the religious, social, political, and economic consequences of racism has devastating consequences for the witness of the church and the integrity of the Gospel it proclaims. The action of some congregations that support racist ideology and offer warm hospitality to racists among their ranks is too dangerous to be ignored. Every congregation has an obligation to play its part in loosening the mortar cementing the brickwork of prejudice and hate.[95] National ecclesial bodies need to take drastic action that obliges each church congregation to take a stand that warns every single congregation of the inadmissible compromise that is inherent in inaction on the racism front.

Perhaps the steps that have been identified above and the suggestion made for the church's resolute action against racism will not represent an adequate response to Willie Jennings' call for a radical transformation of the Christian imagination. Such a transformation would cause a reconfiguration of living spaces into locations where people can imagine new ways of connecting with each other and in which to desire new patterns of social joining. This transformation could contribute to that understanding of life together that is consistent with the church's vision of the reign of God.[96] However, the steps suggested above at least represent a starting point in the struggle against hospitality to racism.

With the deconstruction of the racialized worldview, it will be possible for the churches to develop the capacity to envision a new social order in which inequalities based on assumptions of "race" no longer prevail within the ecclesial family. It will be possible for the churches to exhibit their commitment to realize in themselves, in others, and in our world the joy of loving as Jesus did, of sharing and caring as Jesus did, and of bearing compelling witness to life in community marked by oneness with Christ. Then churches will serve a world in which all people, created in the image of God, may learn from them not only how to live in peace with justice, but also how to engage in fierce competition to outdo one another in showing honor and extending selfless love to each other.

CHAPTER 2

Ethnicity
Establishing Borders of Exclusion

> The concept of "ethnic minorities" . . . is . . . perhaps not as unproblematic as it might, at first sight, seem to be.
>
> Paul Weller[1]

> Official ethnic enumeration is not simply a scientific measurement of objective fact . . . it simultaneously shapes the identities it seeks to capture.
>
> Ann Morning[2]

> [Churches] can help deconstruct myths, stereotypes and prejudices that impede the appreciation and respect of others in their irreducible otherness.
>
> WCC Faith and Order paper[3]

Chapter 1 conveys the affirmation of all human beings belonging to one race—the human race. Yet the term race is understood in various ways. A case in point is the United States of America, where, for example, forms administered by the Census Bureau and the Department of Commerce seek information on people's "race" and also their ethnicity. Some medical clinics also require clients to supply similar information.[4] This tradition has its roots in a customary understanding of the term *race* as a social category that distinguishes people primarily on the basis of external factors, such as the color of their skin.

Unfortunately some people who use the term *race* in terms of phenotype assume that the category reflects a fundamental biological difference between people. When they use the term *ethnicity*, however, they believe this reflects a wider diversity than race. Meanwhile, in parts of the world where popular usage of the term *race* relates to all human beings, people regard *ethnicity* as an accurate and acceptable term to describe the cultural and ancestral background of those they are categorizing. Should the language of ethnicity be preferred over the language of race, when racial categorization is not intended to be an identifier for the entirety of humankind? Should this language displace that of race in certain discourses about difference between people?

After briefly noting the complex nature of the language of ethnicity, this chapter provides an example of the diverse ways in which some Baptists in certain European and North American contexts understand terms such as *ethnic* and *ethnicity*. An exposé of the values that lie behind the use of these terms reveals how the terms may provide a basis for negative and discriminatory characterization of people that is inconsistent with the ethics of *agape*.

If differences in the way people understand and use the terms *ethnic* or *ethnicity* reflect different core valuations of people, what exactly may one claim to constitute the core of the notion of ethnicity? A brief examination of a sample of sociological and anthropological writings on the subject leads to a paradigm for understanding ethnicity. The analysis shows the complexity of the idea of ethnicity. It also reveals the susceptibility of the very descriptor "ethnic" to social differentiation that serves the politics of exclusion.

If the way the word *ethnic* was used at a European Baptist conference and in an American Baptist newspaper elucidates the problematic of ethnic language, and if the notion of ethnicity itself perhaps inherently reflects a tendency to divisiveness, does sacred Scripture model an attitude to ethnicity that tends toward embrace instead of exclusion? A brief foray into the discussion of this issue provides a bridge toward an investigation of the adequacy of the use of the language of ethnicity in Caribbean Theology.

Significant strands of thought in Caribbean Theology utilize a hermeneutics of Incarnation in order to ground the theology's concern for people in the specificity of the historical and cultural situation in the Caribbean. Yet the way this specificity has been delineated in Caribbean Theology may run the risk of overlooking dimensions of life in the region and suggests that limitations mar the vision of ethnicity that the theology espouses.

The discussion that follows claims that most appeals to the ethnicity of Caribbean people who share the heritage of the oppression of plantation history do not give adequate weight to not only the ethnic diversity, but also the religious pluralism of the people of the Caribbean region. In addition, inadequate attentiveness to the gendered understandings of faith in the region may actually obscure rather than illuminate the vision of the theological identity and destiny of the people concerned. A contextual theology that accentuates ethnicity must take adequate cognizance of a range of sociological issues if that theology is to be true to the experience of the people on whose behalf the theology is constructed.

The chapter ends with a conclusion on the usefulness of the language of ethnicity as an index to the identity of a community. If we must refer to people's ethnicity, we may need to do so with great care if our aim is to advance an ethic of community embrace instead of community separation or exclusion.

A Complex Idea

Accounts abound of the changing understandings of the terms *ethnic* and *ethnicity* and their antecedents such as *ethnikos* and *ethnos* in Greek and *ethnicus* in Latin.[5] In the Greek form, the term once signified "heathen" or "pagan." This is the meaning associated with the term in its English usage during the fourteenth century. Later, the term *ethnic* acquired what has been termed "racial" characteristics. By the early 1940s, according to anthropologist Thomas Ericksen, Jews, Italians, Irish, and others deemed inferior to white Anglo-Saxon Protestants in the United States were referred to as "ethnics."[6] Eventually, the term *ethnic* came into popular use and acquired a wide range of meanings.

David Riesman is believed to be the first person to use the English word *ethnicity* in the sense now generally accepted by anthropologists and sociologists.[7] However, seventeen years passed before the term made its first appearance in the *Oxford English Dictionary* in 1972.[8] Ethnicity, like race, is a polysemous term. It was used in different ways to convey a diversity of ideas. Whenever the word appears, care needs to be taken to ensure that one discerns the particular meaning that is being conveyed.

Not surprisingly, multiple definitions of ethnicity exist, and these definitions are not intended to convey the same core understanding.[9] The term "ethnicity" is susceptible to different understandings precisely because it refers to "an intertwining cluster of attributes and not a single cultural characteristic."[10] Furthermore, ethnicity is the subject of multiple disciplines, especially in the social sciences. The body of literature on the subject, written from the perspectives of anthropology, sociology, political economy, and other disciplines, is so extensive that perhaps only specialists can fully envision the vast expanse it covers. The multiplicity of conflicting dimensions of the understanding of ethnicity presents a real challenge for those whose interest in the subject is not academic. As Peruvian sociologist Azril Bacal has said, "The conceptualization of ethnicity remains today as elusive as it is notorious as a public topic."[11]

Over the last forty years, the idea of ethnicity has been receiving greater attention in the literature of missiology and biblical studies.[12] This adds to the complex and varied understanding of the term itself. The diverse approaches to the subject complicate any attempt to present a concise characterization of ethnicity.

The terms *ethnic* and *ethnicity* currently enjoy extensive use within the church, and Christians need to acknowledge the extent to which these terms are problematic. A brief examination of the way these terms have been used in two Baptist publications provides a wealth of evidence to support this assertion.

European Baptist Conference on Ethnic Churches

Especially since 1989, concern has mushroomed among Baptists in Europe over how to relate to the increasing ethnicities reflected in their national population. Not surprisingly, in June 2006 the Division of Mission and Evangelism of the European Baptist Federation (EBF) and the International Baptist Theological Seminary (IBTS) in Prague, Czech Republic, convened a conference on "Ethnic Churches."

The papers presented at the conference appeared in *Ethnic Churches in Europe*, a publication[13] that reveals the diverse ways the term *ethnic churches* is understood. Are these churches communities made up of a single ethnic group? Are these churches that comprise so-called "minorities" exclusively? Is the designation "ethnic churches" a synonym for churches with members who are mostly immigrants? Is the term applicable to churches with members drawn exclusively from the majority population? Does the label "ethnic churches" assign to certain church bodies an identity over against the identity of other churches whose members are a part of the dominant local population group? These are some of the questions to be borne in mind when reading *Ethnic Churches in Europe*. What purpose does the label "ethnic churches" serve?

In his introduction to *Ethnic Churches in Europe*, EBF General Secretary Tony Peck identifies some of the patterns of migration into and across Europe. He explains that the 2006 conference discussed the challenges and opportunities Baptist churches faced owing to "the presence of ethnic groups in Europe." Perhaps with good reason, Peck offers no straightforward definition of *ethnic churches*. Nor does the book he introduces contain a definition of *ethnic churches* that characterizes its various chapters. Indeed, some leading presenters at the conference avoided the descriptor altogether! Meanwhile, in delivering the keynote address at the conference, Paul Weller used the designation with great caution.

Weller attributed the introduction of the expression "ethnic minorities" in Western Europe to the scientific challenge that undermined the biological assumptions of the notion of race.[14] He explained how terms such as *ethnic minority* are used to characterize differences between people and, in the printed text of his address, the expression "ethnic churches" appears always between inverted commas.[15] In one place, Weller actually refers to "so-called ethnic churches."[16]

If Weller was prudent in his use of the expression "ethnic churches," many of the other presenters at the conference did not exhibit the same restraint. It is clear, however, that the speakers, who offered brief reflections on the experience of ministering among distinct population groups in Europe, did not all understand the expression "ethnic churches" in the same way. For example, Jimmy Martin referred to "ethnic, international, and other multi-ethnic churches."[17] Michael Kisskalt mentioned "multi and monoethnic international churches"[18] and "monoethnic immigrant churches."[19] Carmine Bianchi used the term "ethnic churches," but noted that Italian Baptists organized ministry to persons in that category under the rubric of "immigrant church relationships."[20] From Bianchi's presentation one gets the impression that ethnic churches are made up of "Christians from sister churches abroad"[21] and "those left out of the mainstream of society."[22] Meanwhile, Antonio Pires stated that, at one time, the "only ethnic church group" in Portugal was formed by Romani people![23] Yet he asserted: "Ethnic congregations, once established, are to be seen as part of the whole body—the church." These and other churches should "organize common celebrations three or four times a year" for the sake of cementing fellowship and experiencing "the different flavours of Baptist worship."[24]

Endeavoring to offer a carefully crafted description of the situation in his country, David Razzano identified "monoethnic churches among French Baptists"[25] and called for these churches to be given a generous welcome. He warned, however, that concern for these churches need not be at the expense of neglecting "the native population" and those who "belong to French ethnic groups."[26]

Some presenters at the EBF-IBTS conference seemed willing to concede that members of the nonimmigrant population who form the majority group in a country also comprise an ethnic group. However, the churches they form are not usually referred to as "ethnic churches." The reason for this appears to be that that designation is reserved for churches formed by immigrant people or for persons deemed to be minorities in their new residential context.

Terje Aadne from Norway was among those who presented papers on behalf of the Baptist Union in their countries. Aadne provided a significant exception to the overall understanding of what constitutes an ethnic church. He went beyond reticence in the use of the term *ethnic churches* by rejecting the ascription of minority status to those identified by that descriptor. Aadne actually made reference to "ethnic Norwegians,"[27] and he made it abundantly clear that the label "ethnic churches" does not refer exclusively to churches comprising immigrant members. He reserved the term *immigrant churches* for those churches made up of persons who were not ethnic Norwegians.[28]

The use of the expression "ethnic churches" is caught up in the politics of establishing borders and boundaries, identifying separate identities, classifying people over against each other, even where these people share a common bond in Jesus Christ. It appears that the EBF-IBTS conference sought to face squarely the challenge the churches experienced in ministering in their diverse settings. The conference planners employed the expression "ethnic churches" as a device to signify that they were not referring to the churches composed primarily of members of the local majority population.

The Alabama Baptist on Ethnicity

The Alabama Baptist newspaper has a long tradition of commenting on the relationships that should exist among people.[29] Two articles by Bob Terry, distinguished president and editor of *The Alabama Baptist*, exemplify a popular understanding of ethnicity in the United States that may be regarded as highly problematic.[30] How is the term *ethnic* understood in Terry's usage? In the first of his articles, Terry prepares readers of his newspaper for the annual session of the Southern Baptist Convention (SBC) that was to take place in Phoenix, Arizona, in June 2011.[31] Once the SBC Phoenix meeting was over, the June 23, 2011, issue of *The Alabama Baptist* offered retrospective insights into the convention meeting. One common feature of Dr. Terry's two columns is a characterization of ethnic groups as those not made up of people who are classified as "white."

In the preparatory article, Terry wrote:

> The primary business item may be a report from the Executive Committee about how to proactively involve ethnics in convention leadership.... Perhaps it is the upcoming report on involving ethnics in convention leadership that caused this writer to notice the ethnic fellowships meeting in connection with the SBC annual meeting. They are the National African American Fellowship, the Filipino Southern Baptist Fellowship of North America, the Fellowship of Native American Christians and the Southern Baptist Messianic Fellowship.
>
> Among other ethnic groups with which Southern Baptists cooperate are conventions of Hispanic, Korean, Chinese, Romanian and Russian Baptists. There are other growing groups representing Baptists from various African countries ... and others.
>
> Southern Baptists are the most diverse evangelical convention in terms of number of ethnic participants and ethnic groups included. Perhaps it is time for proactive efforts to make sure the rich heritage they bring to SBC life is reflected in leadership roles.

In the retrospective piece, Terry commented on the election of persons he identified as "ethnics" to positions of leadership in the SBC:

> The call for unity, mutual respect and cooperation went beyond entity relationships and SBC/state convention relationships.... The call also included participation of ethnics in convention life. The SBC has been called the most ethnically diverse Protestant denomination in the nation [USA] for more than 20 years. But participation of ethnics on boards and communities has been limited. In Phoenix, messengers approved a plan that provides annual accountability to see if entities are seeking participation and input from ethnics.[32]

Terry continued:

> Over the years, Southern Baptists have adopted many resolutions calling for participation by ethnics, but this is the first time any system of accountability has been put in place.
>
> [Fred] Luter is the first [black person] to serve as first vice president [of the Southern Baptist Convention] and already is being promoted as

a candidate for president when Southern Baptists meet in his hometown in 2012. If he is elected, however, Luter will not be the first ethnic SBC president. That honor goes to immediate past President Johnny Hunt, who is Native American.[33]

In popular American usage, the label "ethnic" seems to reflect a categorization of people not in order to affirm their common belonging in the species *Homo sapiens*, but to highlight the contrast between them and the dominant ethnic group in the United States population. Terry shares with many other writers this understanding of the term *ethnic/s*.[34] He fully grasped, and clearly articulated, the significance of Fred Luter's election, and he reported on it using terminology that reflects the popular understanding of ethnicity by many Christians in the United States. Terry reflected the widespread acceptance of ethnicity as a designation for groups deemed to be made up of people classified as minorities. This understanding of ethnicity appears in some of the sociological literature on ethnicity that originates in the United States, where many people believe that, properly speaking, ethnic groups are "subsections or sub-systems more or less distinct from the rest of the population."[35] Yet, as Thomas Ericksen has explained:

> [M]ajorities and dominant peoples are no less ethnic than minorities. . . . There is power in naming and, more specifically, there is political power inherent in the ability to make a system of social classification relevant. . . . Labels accorded to people as tools of domination would sometimes stick and linger long after the initial conditions of domination had been transformed, creating an often hierarchical grid with particular connotations of "race," "character" and so on, again forming the basis for contemporary ethnopolitics and stereotyping.[36]

The ways in which the word *ethnic* is understood in the EBF-IBTS conference and *The Alabama Baptist* show the extent of their discontinuity with the understanding of ethnicity offered by John Hutchinson and Anthony D. Smith. These scholars define an *ethnic group* as "a named human population with myths of common ancestry, shared historical memories, one or more elements of common culture, a link with a homeland and a sense of solidarity among at least some of its members."[37] This definition reflects the breadth of ideas represented in the varied understandings of the term *ethnicity*.

Ethnicity and Social Differentiation

Christians may wish to pay close attention to the discourse on ethnicity within the social sciences, especially anthropology and sociology. Any suggestion that every single dimension of life is fully and sufficiently explicated within the discourse of theology is wrongheaded. In certain cases, it is possible to integrate insights from social scientific disciplines that reflect on creation with insights gained from what God has revealed through the Scriptures. What may emerge is a holistic understanding that appropriates insights from different perspectives that, taken together, can find their grounding in an understanding of revealed truth. This approach helps an interpreter overcome many of the problems of the "stratigraphic conception of the relations between biological, psychological, social and cultural factors in human life" which, as Clifford Geertz has explained, entails superimposing ideas from contending anthropologies on top of one another without ensuring their consistency or integration within a governing worldview.[38]

On the basis of a thorough analysis of data related to ethnic enumeration in 141 countries, sociologist Ann Morning identifies diverse conceptualizations of ethnicity manifested across the world and clarifies the different usages in various geographical regions. She concludes that, while a United Nations report correctly identifies variety in the operationalization of people's ethnic identity, it is still possible to propose a basic taxonomy of approaches to ethnic enumeration. She provides examples of the ambiguous ways in which identifiers are understood in different cultures:

> What is called "race" in one country might be labeled "ethnicity" in another, while "nationality" means ancestry in some contexts and citizenship in others. Even within the same country, one term can take on several connotations, or several terms may be used interchangeably. . . . One of the most common [distinctions between race, ethnicity and nationality] is the association of ethnicity with cultural commonality—i.e., shared beliefs, values, and practices—while race is seen as revolving around physical . . . commonality.[39]

Setting aside some postmodern approaches that would empty the notion of ethnicity of definitive content, the anthropological literature contains three principal understandings of ethnicity. These may be labeled primordialist, constructivist, and what I will refer to as a synthetic view.

At the core of primordialism, sometimes called essentialism, is the idea that ethnic collectivities are natural and permanent. They are bound together by such ties as race, language, religion, and custom. They are kinship groups that correspond to actual social reality.[40] Ann Morning has noted that an essentialist conception of ethnicity—that is, the idea of ethnicity as something objectively given—seems to mark the understanding reflected, for example, in United States census forms. Significantly, she points out that "only the United States uses separate questions to measure its inhabitants' race versus their ethnicity."[41]

At the core of constructivism, sometimes called instrumentalism, is the belief that ethnic groups are artificial social constructs that have no exact correspondence in actual society. In its many forms, constructivism affirms the boundary-making role of ethnic identities, but it also asserts the fluidity of these identities and the extent to which they are as susceptible to being created as to being abandoned. As Morning has shown, in most of the world where census takers probe people's ethnicity, what is usually reflected is a constructivist understanding of ethnicity—that is, ethnicity as something socially, and so subjectively, developed.[42]

Some anthropologists affirm the constructivist stance, while not abandoning completely the relevance of primordialist elements in the formation of ethnic identity. Fredrik Barth, for example, claims that symbolic "border guards" (such as language and dress, for example) supply boundaries for ethnic groups. Barth notes that, although the boundaries themselves are durable, they are not permanently fixed.[43] For his part, Anthony Smith emphasizes the extent to which ethnic groups are perpetuated through the symbols, myths, and memories that their members treasure.[44] Saskia Wieringa applies the classic essentialist/constructivist divide to her analysis of feminist theory and suggests that "grounding the social in a historicized natural" and applying an essentialist temper to demand the end of oppression may not still prove valuable politically. As a result, while she favors constuctivism, she still refuses to abandon essentialism completely.[45]

This author leans in the direction of constructivism. This implies an understanding of the extent to which terms such as *ethnic* and *ethnicity* need to be understood as mythical concepts that play a major role in social differentiation and may actually serve to promote negative stereotypes that should be abandoned. The term *ethnicity* is mythical insofar as it does not correspond to exact reality. It does not seem feasible scientifically to place people into exact ethnic groups. Put another way, the notion of ethnicity is primarily a metaphorical one. Ethnicity is a constructed identity which often depends on notions of common origins, common heritage, and memories of a shared past. Yet these memories are not always grounded in confirmable historical fact. The Yoruba people are a good example of an ethnic group with contested historical origins. Their origins have been traced, for example, to the people of the Middle East and to the Oyo people of what now is primarily western Nigeria.[46] The "common origins" claimed for Yorubas may best be regarded as consistent with either prevailing perceptions of themselves that Yorubas have or other people's perceptions of who they are. To attribute to them a shared sense of origins is not to allege that the Yorubas who do this rely on uncontested findings of reliable historical research.

Determination of a group's ethnicity rests primarily on subjective criteria rather than on objective external measurement. In some cases people's ethnicity is self-identified. It refers to the group people claim to be their own. In other cases people's ethnicity is assigned by others. In other words, ethnicity may be understood as a sign of a person's self-identity or as a sign of society's classification. In some cases people may disown the ethnicity assigned them. This means that people's ethnicity, whether ascribed or not, does not necessarily reflect their understanding of who they are. Ethnicity is instead about people's affiliation or group classification. Ethnicity pertains to the people's *facere* rather than to their *esse*, their behavior rather than their being. It refers to the construction people make of their own identity or the identity that other people assign them. It is not a classification of some objectively identifiable features that are completely verifiable.

The foregoing may be taken to imply the need for the idea of ethnicity to be deconstructed so that clarity may attend its use as a constructed, and not primarily a biologically-based, identity. When writers refer to Blacks and Native Americans as ethnics, for example, they may not be properly understood to be identifying a clearly defined category into which Blacks and Native Americans can fit with exactness. Their use of the word *ethnics* reflects the proclivity to establish boundaries between people by pointing to what is believed or assumed to constitute something distinctive about them. In some cases the distinctive feature is that these people are not considered to be white.

In the case of groups that are identified as ethnic because their members believe and assert their identity as an ethnic group, this self-identification may actually provide participants with an edifice of meaning to undergird an understanding of the communal existence of these people. The group identification provides the participants with a framework in which they may understand their life in relation to a community in which they share a powerful bond that did not develop out of a historical transaction, such as a consciously negotiated social contract.[47] Affirming one's membership in an ethnic group allows the members to enjoy a sense of rootedness and belonging. This is especially the case when the group members reside in a multiethnic society. Ethnic self-identification offers a means whereby the group may organize to protect and further its own interests. This tends to be noticeable especially when an ethnic group is made up of immigrants.

In cases of enforced or ascribed ethnicity—that is, situations in which those classified as belonging to an ethnic group did not participate in the decision that they should be so identified—ethnic classification may be a device to stigmatize people as belonging to a marginal subgroup, rather than the mainstream, of a society. It may provide the ethnocratic group—that is, the numerical majority group that dominates the society—with a means by which a "negative" valuation of people may be perpetuated. Classifying people as "ethnics" could contribute to their marginalization. It could also contribute to those characterized as such reaffirming internalized feelings of being an oppressed people.

When an ethnocratic out-group defines ethnicity, they may be imposing on groups deemed ethnic a subordinate position vis-à-vis the dominant population, but they may not always realize that this is what they are doing. In the process, however, they may unintentionally do incalculable harm because the descriptor "ethnic" implies a subordinated category to which some people are assigned. Reference to ethnicity may serve to bolster conceptions of difference between people. When people refer to ethnic groups, they may be attempting to establish boundaries between members of one group and those deemed to be different from them in order to establish criteria for social ranking.

On account of these factors, a hermeneutic of suspicion may be appropriate when people appeal to ethnic differentiation. This is likely to be a consideration when those using the language of ethnicity are from the dominant group in a society. These persons often represent powerful social institutions that actually fashion the stereotypes that are developed and nurtured. Sometimes they may be inclined to use the term *ethnic* for less than complimentary reasons. When the assertion of the ethnicity of those regarded as minorities stands side by side with the assumed absence of ethnicity in the dominant population, this may imply the inferiority of those in the minority groups. In other words, relations between the dominant group and so-called ethnic groups are asymmetrical and can easily trigger prejudice and discrimination.

Another danger faced by those who use the language of ethnicity is treating people as captives of an ethnic identity that is regarded as their sole identity. Often the people who are categorized ethnically do actually enjoy simultaneously a range of identities apart from that being referenced when the term *ethnic* is applied to them.[48] Because people may actually hold multiple identities simultaneously, those who assign them to an ethnic group need to recognize that, in doing this, they are actually emphasizing one aspect of people's identity over against, or at the exclusion of, other aspects. In this way they are in danger of judging people, not on the basis of their character and abilities but instead on the basis of their location within a specific group.

In some cases the language of ethnicity is used in such a way as to suggest that ethnicity is *the* major index of a person's personal and social identity. When this happens, stereotyping is a likely outcome. In fact the perception of others primarily in terms of their ethnic identity is likely to cause people to diminish the complexity of other people's multiple identities.

Both the tendency to assign to people one exclusive identity and the practice of prioritizing one feature of a group's identity over other features run the risk of not reflecting a person's identity in terms of his or her uniqueness, inviolable dignity, and priceless worth. This is a danger posed by ethnic identity politics. Ethnic identity can be used as a cloak to disguise prejudice against people who are regarded as different from the dominant group in any society. It may be employed to evince a negative evaluation of others. Members of the "major" group identify those who belong to a so-called "ethnic group" and assert, "They are different from us," without clarifying the precise nature of the difference being referenced.[49]

To summarize, one may argue that ethnic identity is a social construct. It does not describe a fixed and unchanging set of characteristics from which one may always draw defensible conclusions about those characterized by their ethnicity. Members of the Christian community who use the language of ethnicity may wish to bear in mind the risks attending the use of such terms as *ethnic, ethnics*, and *ethnicity*. In what contexts are such terms employed? Are there hidden prejudices that attach themselves to the use of such terms? What function does a person's ethnic identity play in one's overall appraisal of who that person is? Is it true that, despite their professed commitment to God's mission of reconciliation, Christians may actually reveal dishonorable intent when they use the language of ethnicity?

Needless to say, the attention we pay to the subject of ethnicity is not to be understood as an effort to censor anyone for using the language of ethnicity. Certainly, *ethnic* and *ethnicity* are terms that will be in use for many years to come. However, if we must use that language, it may be advisable for us to do so with care. Ethnic terminology should not be employed solely to highlight people's presumed distinctiveness. It should instead be used to secure people's inclusion and participation in the life of the wider community in which they live, work, or play. The importance of this observation will be shown when the subject of Caribbean Theology is discussed later in this book.

Some Biblical Perspectives on Ethnicity

Christians have access to resources that can help them counteract any tendency to use ethnic terminology with the aim of excluding, dominating, or oppressing those deemed outsiders. These biblical and theological resources can aid one's affirmation of people's identities without absolutizing ethnic identity, making it the basis for forming stereotypes that may manifest, or give rise to prejudice. These resources can elucidate our understanding of human identity/identities in such a way that the possible negative implications of the grammar of ethnicity are overcome.

Biblical teaching concerning the creation of all human beings "in the image of God" (Genesis 1:26) provides the basis for a high valuation of every single human being. It is a sign of the sacredness and value of each person. God invests each and every person with intrinsic worth, inviolable dignity, and a solemn calling. All human beings are to recognize an irreplaceable dignity in each other, and the pervasiveness of this dignity means that it is reflected in every single community.

Because the image of God is foundational, relational, and linked with human destiny, it confers an identity on each person that it also confers on all.[50] According to God's design "even the most obscene enemies of human well-being are . . . made in the image of God: they remain human persons, neither to be exonerated from personal responsibility nor to be denied justice and humanity."[51] The image of God in humankind draws people into community, summoning them to respect and care for each other and challenging them to grow into the image of Christ.[52]

There is a sense in which all who are created in the image of God belong to one human family, one race, originating from one ancestor.[53] This family is not privileged by ethnic origin or descent but enjoys its standing through the mercy of God revealed in Jesus Christ. Christians claim that this human family finds its center in Jesus Christ and is drawn into a unified identity through a miracle of grace.[54]

God's impartiality in history is consistent with the divine design in creation. The God who creates all human beings in God's own image, and calls Israel to be a chosen people, is the God who loves all of creation. However, God is one the side of the weak and vulnerable wherever they are found and in whatever guise their oppression takes. No "chosen ones" can count on God when they reject a merciful spirit, eschew empathy, and refuse to practice hospitality. The reason for this is that, in God's inclusive order, ethnicity, social status, gender, and other identifiers do not disqualify people from participating in the new creation that God makes possible.[55] God breaks down dividing walls and enables reconciliation among people.[56]

Biblical teaching on the common creation of all human beings in the image of God and the fact of human existence in a multiplicity of cultures imply people's need to negotiate situations in which one group in a society excludes another from equal status before God. This is one reason why, whenever a biblical text appears to disparage people of certain ethnicities, these passages need to be read in the light of the teaching of the whole of Scripture.[57]

In issuing laws prohibiting mixed marriage, Ezra and Nehemiah used ethnic identity markers precisely as instruments of exclusion.[58] This boundary setting design is inconsistent with the overall thrust of Scripture.

Certain narratives in the Bible appear to predicate the destruction of those deemed to be one's "enemies" and the capture of their land as the will and design of God. Such destruction and conquest may even be presented as the result of divine enabling. Even ethnic cleansing may find justification in some narratives.[59] Such passages need to be read carefully:

> Such "difficult texts can be interpreted through an "internal" critique, by reading them in light of other biblical passages that present a corrective view through their visions of peaceful coexistence, hospitality and the inclusion of strangers. This means that Deuteronomy 7:1–6 cannot be read in isolation from the corrective that comes from Deuteronomy 10:17–19.[60]

Preaching from some problematic biblical texts that appear to be supportive of violence against others is fraught with enormous challenges. Fortunately, published resources exist that may assist preachers in their quest to deliver sermons based on such texts of Scripture.[61]

Human beings and the whole of creation are caught up in new possibilities when people's lives are ordered according to God's will. In this situation, one needs to recognize, acknowledge, and face the dangers involved when one is applying biblical teaching in discipleship programs that provide guidance for believers in Christ.

The God who is the author and lover of creation has set firmly in place a design that should inspire respectful and loving interpersonal relationships and peaceful social coexistence. Moreover, the God whom Jesus discloses crosses boundaries and violates well-established social and cultural norms to affirm those who are pushed to the periphery of any society that regards them as outcasts or outsiders unworthy of benefiting from personal and social solidarity.[62]

Framers of contextual theologies need to embrace multiple aspects of the society in which theologizing is being undertaken to ensure that the extensiveness of divine love and the wideness of God's mercy are reflected in their "definition of the situation."[63] This is a lesson that those who continue to frame Caribbean Theology are beginning to come to terms with. When they look back on the development of a theology that is related to the life situation, history, and challenges faced by the people of the Caribbean, they are seeking to identify the people with and for whom the theology is being developed. The way biblical texts are appropriated and the local population is perceived are critical for a contextual theology that can contribute to true human development in a community marked by justice for all.

Using the Language of Ethnicity

Christians have much in common as human beings created in the image of God (see Genesis 1:26–27) and as persons being transformed in the image of Christ (see Romans 8:29). They should locate whatever discernible differences they observe within this twin context. In this perspective, a diminishment of the penchant to employ ethnicity as a language of exclusion should become evident.

The ethnicity of any group always should be set within the context of the other social identities that a group enjoys. By this means, the appeal to a wider range of images will more accurately portray the identity or identities developed. One should not simply place people in imagined communities and then make sweeping generalizations about them based on their assigned group identity. If a single identity is assigned to persons at the expense of their other social identities, caricatures will be produced on which people can ground the prejudices reflected in their use of the language of ethnicity.

It is noteworthy that people's social identity is not fixed, static, and stable. Instead, these identities are constantly being formed and reshaped. Created in and for community, people interact with each other, and they are influenced both by one another and by changing historical circumstances. In this process they keep negotiating their identities, "remaking" themselves.[64]

Christians need to commit to overcoming the negative implications of the use of ethnic classification that may not even be the primary self-identity of people belonging in a group.

Yet it must be admitted that the language of ethnicity, however diverse and problematic its use may be, is likely to persist for years to come. It is important, then, that the term does not become a synonym for race understood in biological terms. Otherwise, the use of terms like *ethnic, ethnicity*, and *ethnic group* may end up supplying fodder for political linguistics.[65] Furthermore, the limitations of the language of ethnicity need always to be remembered, especially when the discussion of appropriate contextual theologies takes place.

It is entirely unclear whether the language of ethnicity as a replacement for the language of race does in fact solve the problem of conceptualizing otherness in community-destroying ways. From this, one may conclude that, if ethnic classification is to be utilized, it should be placed intentionally in the service of inclusion and not exclusion. A special effort will need to accompany the use of the language of ethnicity to ensure that it is employed for the constructive purpose of healthy, just, and inclusive community development. As Harry Lucenay once wrote, "Learning to work with diversity creates the setting in which God's symphony of humanity can audition."[66] Is there a better context that nurtures this value than the Holy Communion, which is the focus of the next chapter?

CHAPTER 3

Communion
Celebrating Inclusive Community

[In the Lord's Supper], God . . .
crosses divisions and differences to invite
each of us to full participation in life with God.

Andrew Packman[1]

We cannot be guests of the Crucified without living the
solidarity he practiced. So the church is celebrating the
meal unworthily if it does not live in solidarity; it is belying
the hope offered to the hungry and the oppressed.

Horton Davies[2]

The Eucharist is the symbol of unity—unity in the church and
unity of humankind as a whole, symbolizing the dimension
of hope and the full stature of the body of Christ.

Edourd Boné[3]

The Lord's Supper . . . is a performative act of common prayer
by a covenant community that recalls as a memorial of the
Father the unique sacrifice of the Son and invokes God's abiding
and eschatological presence through the Spirit. And as such
it prefigures and indeed hastens the very future it signifies.

Curtis Freeman[4]

> Solidarity . . . finds its first source
> in the sacraments and its first expression in
> prayer [in the works of the early church fathers].
>
> *Igino Giordani*[5]

Are resources available to help the church overcome the boundaries Christians construct using racial and ethnic categories? In this chapter, a claim is made for the capacity of a eucharistic hermeneutic to help Christians overcome the potentially divisive effects of the language we employ when addressing the subject of human identity and diversity. The expressive and instrumental functions of Holy Communion are a source for the human solidarity that precludes the exclusion of the stranger.

In keeping with divine volition and design, every single human being is made "in the image of God" (Genesis 1:27; cf. Psalm 8:5–8). God invests in each person an inviolable dignity and an inestimable worth and renders them creatures bound for community, marked by mutuality and interdependence, and called to love one another. This reality is part of the mystery of God's creation. It is a sign of the architecture of grace that undergirds human existence.

Yet many persons claim for themselves the "right" to classify people, using criteria of their own choosing. In this process, they frequently employ the language of division. Some of the terms they use—such as *race* and *ethnicity*—are fraught with conceptual imprecision. These expressions are categories of the imagination; they are images that function as identity markers to establish boundaries within the human community. When Christians use these highly freighted terms, they should try to ensure that what they say is congruent with biblical teaching concerning the value God places on people and the relations God expects among people. This way the content of their language will reflect the love and respect for others that is consistent with the meta-narrative revealed in God's creation and the divine self-manifestation in Jesus Christ.

Jesus Christ is present and at work in the church's sacrament/ordinance[6] that involves a shared meal. This commemorative meal that most Christians enact is not given an exact name in the Scriptures of the church, where Paul refers to it as the *kuriakon deipnon*, the Lord's Supper.[7] Holy Scripture provides a firm foundation for the name *Eucharist*, although Ignatius and Justin Martyr were the first to use that term to identify the worship event.[8] Besides the Lord's Supper and the Eucharist, this sacred meal is also called Holy Communion, Breaking of Bread, Divine Liturgy, and the Mass.[9] The extensiveness of the literary corpus dealing with this sacrament is related to the importance of this multidimensional event that lies at the very center of the corporate worship of the church.

Holy Communion has much to teach believers in Christ about human identity. It exposes the meaning and some of the implications of the restored identity that God gives to Christians. God creates all human beings in God's own image, but in Jesus Christ, who embodies the very image of God, humankind and the whole creation are reconciled to God. Through the Holy Spirit a new creation emerges. As Paul states, "If anyone is in Christ, there is a new creation. Everything old has passed away: see everything has become new! All this is from God who reconciled us to himself through Christ and has given us the ministry of reconciliation" (2 Corinthians 5:17–18).

Our divided world needs a theological anthropology that affirms the commonality shared by all human beings whom God has made. It also needs to take into account the significance of the redeemed community as a sign of the new creation.[10] Those who experience this new creation are able to overcome the possible negative perception of otherness that is sometimes expressed in racial or ethnic classification.

In this chapter, the Lord's Supper is presented as primarily a worship event in which the past, present, and future collide in the formation and nourishment of Christian identity. By harvesting an insight from the field of social anthropology, showing the way in which community meals both form and shape group identity,[11] the expressive and instrumental role in identity formation that community meal events played in ancient Israel and in Greco-Roman society is demonstrated. Then, through consideration of certain dimensions of the Eucharist, including some of its socio-ethical implications, a case is made for the possibility of a proper understanding of Holy Communion contributing significantly in helping churches overcome the negative aspects of the ethnic divisions that exist within and among them and in the contexts where they serve. Christians may need to develop a more adequate appreciation of the capacity of the Lord's Supper to help them overcome the limitations caused by their racial and ethnic identities.

Contributors to the literature on Holy Communion tend to emphasize one of the various aspects of this liturgical event. As the landmark ecumenical convergence text on baptism, Eucharist, and ministry states, the meaning of the event may be grasped in the confluence of a number of themes identified as thanksgiving to the Father, *anamnesis* or memorial of Christ, invocation of the Spirit, communion of the faithful, and meal of the kingdom.[12] Each of these emphases is integral to the meaning of the Lord's Supper, and all of them are essential for a comprehensive understanding of this multistranded community event.[13]

The Meaning of Eating Together

What meaning and significance may one attach to events where people gather to share a common meal? As anthropologists such as Mary Douglas, Maurice Bloch, and Louis Dumont have shown, commensality—the action of intentionally eating together—both reflects and contributes to the formation of people's identity in their social context. Communal meal events express the shared values that people hold. They also provide some clues that elucidate our understanding of the social implications of common participation in a meal.[14]

In her seminal essay, "Deciphering a Meal," British social anthropologist Mary Douglas explores the significance of a meal in its social context. She explains:

> If food is treated as a code, the messages it encodes will be found in the pattern of social relations being expressed. The message is about different degrees of hierarchy, inclusion and exclusion, boundaries and transactions across the boundaries.[15]

Douglas shows how meals frame the meaning of the gathering in which they take place. In them a line is drawn between intimacy and distance to reveal that "each meal is a structured social event which structures others in its own image."[16]

Douglas is not alone in her explanation of the grammar of meals as events that convey social meaning and have social implications. In his *magnum opus* on the caste system in India, Louis Dumont[17] analyzes the role played by an understanding of hierarchy that is grounded in a religious worldview with its codified teaching on purity and impurity.[18] In this context, Dumont discusses the meaning of rules governing human contact in India and notes that "rules concerning food permit certain relations between castes."[19] Drawing on his own research, as well as studies done by others,[20] Dumont shows how physical bodily proximity and participation in a common meal signify, among other things, the close relationship existing between participating diners. He claims that "one can scarcely ever eat side by side with any but one's equals,"[21] and he explains that the frontiers of commensality lie within the boundaries created by traditional values adopted by caste members.[22]

The conclusions about commensality that British anthropologist Maurice Bloch has drawn are not inconsistent with those of Douglas and Dumont. In his essay "Commensality and Poisoning,"[23] Bloch makes an assertion that now seems to represent the consensus of social anthropologists:

> In all societies, sharing food is a way of establishing closeness. . . . Commensality . . . is thus one of the most powerful operators of the social process. . . . The sharing of food is, and is always seen to be, in some way or other, the sharing of that which will cause, or at least maintain, a common substance among those who commune together.[24]

He goes on to say, "[It] expresses, and is also believed to cause, the bodily unification of persons who eat together."[25] Bloch admits that variety marks the cultural forms and meanings of commensality. Furthermore, he believes that it is not possible to account fully for this variety in some universal human predisposition.[26] He claims, however, that one should not overlook the strong regularities in commensality since they both reflect the common bond that people share and serve as a mechanism that creates that bond.[27]

Commensality has deep social significance. It offers insights into how social bonds are established, maintained, regenerated, or reappropriated through ritual actions involving persons belonging to a group that claims bonds of spiritual and social solidarity. Though not being an anthropologist himself, Jordan Rosenblum sums up well the sentiment of many anthropologists when he states:

> With whom you eat is a powerful statement about your identity, whether you live in 210 C.E. or 2010 C.E. Breaking bread is a social language that operates under the assumption that commensality is a practice that results in social digestion—breaking groups into smaller social units. . . . [C]ommensality leads to social intimacy and identity.[28]

Meal Events in Ancient Israel

The Hebrew Bible contains many accounts of meal events. These narratives provide a basis for conclusions one may draw concerning the religious and social significance of commensality in ancient Israel.[29] Scholars such as Isidore Epstein, George Foote Moore, and Peter Altmann have provided windows into the discernment of the meaning and value of communal meal events in ancient Israel.

Epstein has argued that, as ritual meal events, three annual festivals in ancient Israel—the Feast of Unleavened Bread, the Feast of Weeks, and the Feast of Tabernacles—were meant to express Israel's vocation to be God's holy people. "Holiness," Epstein says, "is the keynote of the "Appointed Seasons,"[30] and the idea of holiness goes to the heart of the relationship between the people of ancient Israel and their God. It also includes an understanding of the relationships the Hebrews shared with each other. The three great annual festivals were all meal events, and they served both identity-affirming and solidarity-building functions among people who regarded themselves as blessed to share a special identity as God's holy people.

One way in which the ritual life of ancient Israel fulfilled its function in defining and reinforcing identity was in the inclusion of actions to help the people remember a shared past and celebrate their common hopes. Identifying this feature of festivals in ancient Israel, George Foote Moore explains that, by remembering and celebrating together in cultic observances involving meals, the Israelites were galvanized into "an essential oneness."[31] Ritual meal-sharing in ancient Israel, he explains, may be understood as implying certain beliefs about people's relationship with God and with each other. It may also imply certain assumptions about how those beliefs are established and maintained.

In more recent studies of festive meals in the ancient world, scholars continue to unveil elements of identity politics that characterize such events in Israelite and in other cultures. Peter Altmann, for example, shows how festive meals described in the Hebrew Bible bear witness to the role that commensality plays in expressing and forging relationships among people in community. Altmann states that, in the Hebrew Bible, "the company one keeps—or lack thereof—while eating and drinking greatly influences a person's identity." Celebratory meals, he says, are occasions that play a role in the organization of society.[32]

Turning to the ritual meals described in Deuteronomy 12–26, Altmann shows how these served to solidify group belonging, depicting Israel as a unified people. Observing that communal meal events also provided "an enhanced sense of belonging" in cultures surrounding ancient Israel, Altmann suggests that this tradition helps readers understand what is happening in these celebratory feasts. He describes what he terms "symbolically freighted feasting events" in Akkadian, Ugaritic, and Babylonian circles to show that people perceived their deities as sponsors or hosts at such meals. Altmann suggests that the writer of Deuteronomy makes use of "the image of the festival meal on display in the mythological and royal celebrations found in the *Enuma Elish* and the *Baal Cycle*—to name two prominent examples—and transforms it into a feast provided by Yahweh."[33]

The identity forming and preserving functions of communal meal events in ancient Israel seem reasonably evident, and it is not surprising that similar functions can be detected in communal meals in early Christianity.

Meal Events in Early Christianity[34]

Linkages have been found in the understanding of the social significance of commensal practice among the people of ancient

Israel, in Rabbinical Judaism, during the first three centuries of the Common Era, and in contemporary Jewish culture.[35] Meal events in early Christianity also reflect the influence of traditions emerging in the Greco-Roman world, which was the cradle of early Christianity. Analyzing Greek dining tradition, Oswyn Murray is among those who have shown that "forms of eating and drinking . . . reflect and reinforce the social system in a variety of complex ways: they also create and maintain a variety of cultural values."[36]

After investigating the relationship between the meal traditions reflected in the New Testament and those in the surrounding cultures, Dennis Smith, Fergus King, and Gillian Feeley-Harnik[37] have focused attention on the interrelationship between the various traditions.

In probing the continuity between the Lord's Supper and banquet patterns in the first centuries of the Common Era, Dennis Smith shows how ritual meals expressed community-affirming and community-sustaining values. He also explains how these meals helped define social boundaries and imposed a social-ethical code.[38] Smith argues, "Whom one dines with defines one's placement in a larger set of social networks. . . . [T]he social code of the banquet represents a confirmation and ritualization of the boundaries that exist in a social situation."[39]

Smith suggests that the banquet reflected an already existing bond. To welcome someone at one's table was to affirm that person's participation in one's social network. The banquet "provided a significant means for one's status in society to be formally recognized and acknowledged."[40]

The banquet was also an occasion for social bonding. The act of dining together, Smith argues, was believed to create a bond between the diners who shared common food and ate at a common table or from a common dish. The banquet also brought participants into relations involving certain mutual obligations. As Smith explains, sharing a meal created "a sense of ethical obligation of diners toward one another. . . . People understood that those who dined together were to be treated equally."[41] He adds, "The banquet was a social institution of such significance in the ancient Mediterranean social world that it was commonly utilized by all sorts of distinct social groups as an effective means for confirming and celebrating their self-consciousness as a community."[42]

By focusing on such traditions as the Greek *Symposium*, the Roman *Convivium*, eating in guilds and clubs, and dining with the deity, Fergus King provides a succinct summary of research findings on commensality in the Greco-Roman world.[43] Although King's intention is to map the pattern of inculturation reflected in the narratives of the Lord's Supper in the New Testament, he shows clearly the role that meals played in identity politics in the Greco-Roman world. King identifies resemblances between Judaic practice and Holy Communion and notes that, in terms of actions during the meal, Jesus may be identified with the *paterfamilias* of the Passover or the Messiah/Priest of the Qumran Essene meal. King adds: "That bread and cup are shared without distinction on the grounds of status or hierarchy gives a very different feel to the actions being carried out, and their significance for the participants in the meal."[44] He draws attention to the complex practice of ranking that characterized the meals for guilds, clubs, and associations,[45] and he asserts, as among the "common concerns of Christian and Graeco-Roman rituals . . . the enhancement of group identity."[46]

Gillian Feeley-Harnik discovered similar commensal functions when she probed "the eating habits of contemporary Jews and gentiles as exhibited in documents written or in use during the Greco-Roman period in Palestine and the diaspora."[47] She notes, however, that, while the Passover was a celebration of kinship and nationhood, the Eucharist that centers on Jesus' sacrifice symbolized the death of family and polity and the democratization of the covenant that now included all humanity.[48] Commensality and covenant are connected, and table fellowship is "synonymous with fellowship in all aspects of life."[49] In Feeley-Harnik's understanding, commensality actually confirms or even constitutes kinship.[50]

Drawing upon narratives in the Hebrew Bible, Feeley-Harnik shows the adverse effects of the refusal to share in a common meal. "Refusing to eat together," she asserts, "severs . . . relationship (see 1 Samuel 20:34). Those who do not eat or drink together are without any obligations to one another, if not actually enemies. . . . [T]he worst kind of traitor is one with whom one has shared food (see Psalm 41:9; Obadiah 1:7; Matthew 26:21; Mark 14:17; Luke 22:21; John 13:18, 24–27)."[51]

The New Testament, like the Hebrew Bible, provides a wealth of narrative involving meal events that is comparable to the literature reflecting the Greek and Roman traditions. As Markus Barth has noted, meals play a conspicuous role in approximately one-fifth of the sentences in the Gospel of Luke and in the Acts of the Apostles.[52] Luke's Gospel provides accounts of Jesus dining at Levi's house (5:27–32); at the house of Simon the Pharisee (7:36–50); at Bethsaida (9:10–17); in the home of a Pharisee (11:37–54; 14:15–24); and in the home of Zacchaeus (19:1–10). After his resurrection, Jesus appeared at a shared meal with the travelers on the road to Emmaus (24:13–35), and he also invited his disciples to a meal including fish (24:36–49). Jesus' meal practice led his distracters to identify him with his fellow diners and thus call him a glutton and drunkard (7:34).[53]

The Lord's Supper, when it is interpreted in the context of the ancient Near East and the Greco-Roman world from which the early church emerged, may be described as a meal that defines and strengthens the identity of followers of Christ. When participants draw near to the Lord's Table, in a setting where Jesus himself is believed to be present as host, they realize their identity as persons incorporated into the body of Christ, the church. Therefore, from the beginning, those who were baptized were soon led to the Communion Table, where they would have the opportunity to share in this special communal meal for the first time. By this means, the church signified the new standing of the believer as one who had been incorporated into Christ and had become a member of the body of Christ. Not surprisingly, therefore, the Lord's Supper serves as the occasion when communicants share one loaf and drink from one cup as an expression of their oneness in Christ. Furthermore, these believers are nourished at the Lord's Table so that they may grow into Christ, realizing ever more fully their relationship with God and each other and the moral and social obligations that this relationship implies.

The Lord's Supper and Christian Identity

In corporate worship, the gathered community of believers experiences a dynamic encounter in which they remember, identify with, and celebrate foundational events of their faith. As followers of Christ, those assembled for worship express solidarity with those who were with their Lord at the Last Supper on the night of the his betrayal. They affirm their participation, through their baptism, in Jesus' death and resurrection. They acknowledge that they are part of the community formed by the Holy Spirit in response to these historic salvific events. They also recognize their belonging in the wider world, which is the mission field on which God in Christ sends them in the power of the same Spirit.

Stanley Grenz addresses clearly the crucial role the church plays in transmitting the salvation story from generation to generation, thereby mediating to its members "the framework for the formation of personal identity and values." He continues:

> Central to this identity shaping task is the recital of the church's constituting narrative. . . . The church functions as a community of memory and hope, linking the present to the past and the future.

> Within this process, the church's rites play a crucial role. These acts are an indispensable means whereby the group is placed ritually into the narrative that constitutes them as a community. . . . [B]aptism and the Lord's Supper serve as symbols of the relationship of believers to God and to one another.[54]

In Holy Communion, followers of Christ do not only identify with past events. They also express their keen anticipation of a future for which they long. In the Lord's Supper, believers anticipate and enter into the meal of the kingdom[55] that is revealed in its fullness when creation is renewed at the end of this age.[56] When they share the bread and the cup of Holy Communion, Christians bear witness to the heavenly kingdom by celebrating their common life in Christ and their common participation in God's mission. They publicly acknowledge the fellowship they enjoy in and with God, and they affirm that this fellowship is fully realized only at the end of the age. If heaven is a place of communion and genuine intimacy,[57] in the Lord's Supper heaven and earth meet as human beings encounter the past, present, and future converging in the presence of God.

In this perspective, the Lord's Supper is an anamnesis (remembrance) in a twofold sense. It is an anamnesis in the sense that it draws upon the memory of the formative events of the Christian story. It is an anamnesis also in the sense that it is an entering into the future, an entering into the experience of the new age.[58] Worshippers recognize that Christ is present among them, making efficacious the action accomplished once for all on the cross and in the resurrection. The risen Christ, who is present in the Eucharist, unites participants to himself, thereby forging a Holy Communion.[59] In the Lord's Supper, the present is filled with memories of the Lord's self-offering and with hope for the future fulfillment of the promise of the kingdom. But it is also charged with the enjoyment of Christ's living and active presence here and now. In Holy Communion "the past, the present and the future coincide. . . . All that Jesus Christ means in his person and redemptive work is brought forth from history to our present experience which is also a foretaste of the future fulfilment of God's unobstructed reign."[60]

When Christians share in this Holy Communion, they commune with one another in and with their Lord. They realize in the event itself how, as one body in Christ, they participate in fellowship with believers of all the ages—past, present, and future. As Jean-Jacques von Allmen puts it, "The Supper is a two-fold communion; it unites Christ and the Church [and] it unites Christians to one another. These two aspects are indissoluble, the latter being determined and also implied by the former."[61]

Participants in the Lord's Supper encounter and celebrate the Lord's presence, and they receive a potent reminder—and a needed confirmation—of who they have become in Christ Jesus. Authentic sharing in the Eucharist includes discernment of Christ's presence in the worshipping community, forming followers of Christ in their identity and for their vocation. With the General Baptists of the late seventeenth century Britain, participants realize that

> as they [the people of ancient Israel] had the manna to nourish them in the wilderness to Canaan; so have we the sacraments, to nourish us in the church, and in our wilderness-condition.[62]
>
> The supper of the Lord Jesus [is] to be observed in his church . . . for the perpetual remembrance, and showing forth the sacrifice of himself in his death; and the confirmation of the faithful believers in all the benefits of his death and resurrection, and spiritual nourishment and growth in him; sealing unto them . . . to be a band and pledge of communion with him, and an obligation of obedience to Christ . . . as also of our communion and union each with other, in the participation of this holy sacrament.[63]

Holy Communion is a banquet for all whose identity has been transformed, and who are being nurtured, by the grace of the Father, through the love of the Son, in the fellowship of the Holy Spirit. Diners share a meal with the risen Christ as the disciples did with Jesus in the post-resurrection period. They also share a meal in Christ insofar as the Eucharist is a participation in the body and blood of Christ.[64] Not surprisingly, therefore, *Baptism, Eucharist and Ministry*, often referred to as *BEM*, states: "The eucharistic communion with Christ who nourishes the life of the Church is at the same time communion within the body of Christ which is the Church. The sharing in one bread and the common cup in a given place demonstrates and effects the oneness of the sharers with Christ and with their fellow sharers in all times and places."[65]

The Holy Communion, Community Formation, and Failure

Embodied rituals, such as the Lord's Supper, are solidarity-building events employing "common human capacities [of] motion, sound, [and] taste." When they are performed in settings in which cultural boundaries are crossed, they promote "consciousness of kind . . . [and] can therefore bond persons to one another and create new communities."[66] Conceived in the perspective of identity formation, nurture, and maintenance, Holy Communion is a community meal with expressive and instrumental functions that can help the church overcome the boundaries Christians construct using racial and ethnic categories.

Unfortunately, Holy Communion, which is meant to be a symbol of the unity God gives to followers of Jesus Christ, has become a tragic sign of the disunity of the church. This scandal influences the church's resolve to overcome disunity and provides a basis for the commitment of the Faith and Order Commission of the World Council of Churches (WCC) to years of work spent exploring the reasons behind the lack of agreement around significant aspects of the church's life and proposing ways to possibly overcoming the differences that are divisive.

At their meeting in Lima, Peru, in 1982, the WCC Commission on Faith and Order affirmed *BEM* as a text representing the churches' doctrinal convergence. Since that time this landmark ecumenical text has played a seminal role in almost all subsequent major discussion of the issues the text addresses.[67] Notwithstanding this, controversy continues to swirl around a common understanding of the meaning of the Lord's Supper and of the constitution of a ministry that is competent to superintend its liturgical observance. These controversies prevent Christians belonging the Roman Catholic, Orthodox, Anglican, Protestant, Evangelical, and Pentecostal churches from always being ready to admit to the Lord's Table practicing Christians who declare faith in Jesus Christ as Lord, are baptized into the life of the triune God, but who associate with churches not in full communion with those in their own ecclesial tradition. Tragically, some believe that the churches have failed to achieve the doctrinal consensus, or at least a sufficient convergence, on which to predicate common sharing at the Lord's Table.

The separation of people at the Table of the Lord is occasioned, not only by concern for different understandings of what constitutes doctrinal orthodoxy on the Eucharist, but also by the distinctions that arise among people based on their ethnicity. In some parts of the United States, for example, African Americans have been prevented from assembling for worship with whites or else were encouraged to find venues where they could worship by themselves. In some cases, white Christians provided incentives to seduce black Christians into forming separate communities that meet in venues not shared by whites.[68] Hardly can African Americans be harshly judged for refusing to abandon corporate worship of God or surrender their place in the church. That so many millions of them still call the church their spiritual home is nothing short of a miracle worthy of celebration.

The tradition of separate gatherings for corporate worship by people of different ethnic origins has persisted in certain communities in the United States. With the remarkable ethnic diversity that characterizes the country, it is now customary for people to say that the divisions in the church in the US appear to be most evident on a Sunday morning when, separated by their ethnicities, many Christians attend churches where they celebrate the Lord's Supper without any sense that this may reflect a scandalous failure on the church's part.[69] T. B. Maston has credibly stated:

> How tragic it would be if the churches became "the last bulwark of racial segregation"! What a paradox if secularism and secular institutions "outchristianize Christianity"! It has frequently been said that eleven o'clock on Sunday morning is the most segregated hour of the week. This is close enough to the truth to embarrass many of our churches and to give Christians an uneasy conscience.[70]

Yet, as *BEM* shows, churches around the world are growing in their awareness of the identity-forming function of the sacraments. Concerning baptism, *BEM* declares, for example, that through baptism "Christians are brought into union with Christ, with each other and with the Church of every time and place. Our common baptism, which unites us to Christ in faith, is thus a basic bond of unity" ("Baptism" §6).[71] *BEM* also states clearly that baptism "initiates the reality of the new life given in the community of the Holy Spirit" and "gives participation in the community of the Holy Spirit" ("Baptism" §7).

The identity-shaping function of the Eucharist is also affirmed in *BEM*, which presents God at work in the eucharistic gathering, teaching and nourishing the Church ("Eucharist" §29). "In the eucharistic meal," *BEM* states, "in the eating and drinking of bread and wine, Christ grants communion with himself. God himself acts, giving life to the body of Christ and renewing every member ("Eucharist" §2).[72]

Furthermore, as referenced earlier, *BEM* makes clear that

> the eucharistic communion with Christ who nourishes the life of the Church is at the same time communion within the body of Christ which is the Church. The sharing in one bread and the common cup in a given place demonstrates and effects the oneness of the sharers with Christ and with their fellow sharers in all times and places. It is in the Eucharist that the community of God's people is fully manifested ("Eucharist" §19).

As "communion of the faithful," the Lord's Supper is a location where God is at work. "Through the Eucharist the all-renewing grace of God penetrates and restores human personality and dignity" ("Eucharist" §20). The clear implication and corollary of this is the obligation that Christians love one another.

As with the unity of the Father and the Son reflected in John 17, the unity of those sharing in the Lord's Supper is a unity founded on love. Holy Communion is a feast of love and, as Anabaptist theologian Pilgram Marpek states, "If love is missing, then Christ's example is completely counterfeited, and the communion cannot be referred to as the Supper of the Lord."[73] Within the fellowship of the Lord's Supper, the relation between the memorial of Christ and the washing of the disciples' feet signifies both the mysterious unity Christians share and their mission of loving service both within and beyond the immediate context of the church.[74]

Because love is incumbent and makes huge demands on all members of the church in their relations to each other, in *A Declaration of Faith of English People Remaining at Amsterdam in Holland,* pioneer Baptist Thomas Helwys and his followers insist:

> That the members off evrie Church or Congregacion ought to knowe one another, that so they may performe all the duties off love one towards another both to soule and bodie. . . . And especialle the Elders ought to knowe the whole flock, whereof the HOLIE GHOST hath made them overseers. . . . And therefore a Church ought not to consist off such a multitude as cannot have particular knowledge one off another.[75]

In Christian worship, fellowship in speech and action around word and table expresses and generates the passion that unleashes among the participants a loving concern for each other and a readiness to fulfill the obligations of neighbor love in their communities. As Angel Mendez Montoya has observed, "Food is . . . political: it is a practice that imagines divine sharing as the locus (spatial and temporal) of 'holy communion' with one another and with God. . . . This eating is . . . a recognition or awareness that God loves and generously shares divinity in spite of and in the midst of sin."[76] If the Eucharist as "communion of the faithful" is a location where God is at work, it is also a context in which Christians are strengthened for their vocation of practitioners of *philadelphia* and of responsible engagement in the world.

The Holy Communion and the Mission of the Church

Some of the consequences of the solidarity-creating function of the Holy Communion were affirmed at the World Conference on Mission and Evangelism convened by the Commission on World Mission and Evangelism (CWME) in Melbourne, Australia, in 1980.[77] Section III of the *Melbourne Conference Report* declares that incorporation into Christ through the work of the Holy Spirit "is the greatest blessing of the kingdom, and the only abiding ground of [the church's] missionary activity in the world."[78] It describes the Eucharist as "a witness to the kingdom of God and an experience of God's reign."

It also explains that the Eucharist "gives life to Christians so that they may be formed in the image of Christ and so become effective witnesses to him."[79]

The CWME report states credibly that, in their living out of eucharistic witness, Christians take a stand against poverty, discrimination, and other forms of injustice:

> Where a people is being harshly oppressed, the Eucharist speaks of the exodus or deliverance from bondage. Where Christians are rejected or imprisoned for their faith, the bread and wine become the life of the Lord who was rejected by men but has become "the chief stone of the corner." . . . Where discrimination by race, sex or class is a danger for the community, the Eucharist enables the people of all sorts to partake of one food and be made one people. . . . God feeds his people as they celebrate the mystery of the Eucharist so they may confess in word and deed that Jesus Christ is Lord, to the glory of God the Father.[80]

The life of the Christian community is formed and shaped by its members' one baptism and the common sharing at the Lord's Table. Baptism and the Lord's Supper nurture the church's identity and form the church for its mission. Part of this mission is the declaration of the Gospel, that is, the retelling of the story of Jesus whom God sent into the world to gather all creation under the lordship of Christ.[81] United with Christ in baptism, and nourished again and again at the Lord's Table, Christians are equipped to bear witness to the gracious work of the triune God who, through Christ, reconciles human beings and the whole of creation to God. Faithfulness to God requires the church to bear witness to what the Father has accomplished through the Son and to call everyone to baptism and the life of faith. This mission also includes the church's vocation to live in solidarity with the poor through a ministry of advocacy, caring and sharing.[82]

Holy Communion has immense social justice implications.[83] If the Johannine account of the washing of the disciples' feet is associated with Jesus' last supper, it models how loving and serving others flow from the Lord's Supper. Not surprisingly, the apostle Paul expressed concern over the failure of the church in Corinth to understand the social implications of the Eucharist:

> In the first place, I hear that when you come together as a church, I hear that there are divisions among you; and to some extent I believe it. Indeed, there have to be factions among you, for only so will it become clear who among you are genuine. When you come together, it is not really to eat the Lord's supper. For when the time comes to eat, each of you goes ahead with your own supper, and one goes hungry and another becomes drunk. What! Do you not have homes to eat and drink in? Or do you show contempt for the church of God and humiliate those who have nothing? What should I say to you? Should I commend you? In this matter I do not commend you![84]

The Eucharist, *BEM* explains, calls for a solidarity that involves "responsible care of Christians for one another and the world ("Eucharist," §21). From the beginning, therefore, the church has acknowledged that its participation in the life of the triune God includes its obligation to care for people in need. Those who lacked sufficient material possession were given the assistance they needed:

> Now the whole group of those who believed were of one heart and soul, and no one claimed private ownership of any possessions, but everything they owned was held in common. With great power the apostles gave their testimony to the resurrection of the Lord Jesus, and great grace was upon them all. There was not a needy person among them, for as many as owned lands or houses sold them and brought the proceeds of what was sold. They laid it at the apostles' feet, and it was distributed to each as any had need.[85]

From the earliest centuries of the church's life, the social justice implications of Holy Communion have been reflected in the literature the church has produced. Again and again, in descriptions of the church's corporate worship, and in examples of its preaching and teaching ministry, followers of Christ have been reminded that their obligation to care for others is a postulate of participation in the Lord's Supper.

During the first six centuries of the Common Era, the "church fathers" understood the connection between the Eucharist and the daily life of the members of the Christian community. They especially emphasized the importance of concern for social harmony and care for the poor as duties implied by the Eucharist. The contents of the Law and the Prophets, the New Testament witness to the teaching and example of Jesus, and the life of the Early Church are identified as sources for the Christian obligation to care for the poor.[86]

The *Didache*,[87] which is perhaps a mid-second century compilation, insists that the Eucharist is only for those who are baptized.[88] It reflects the church's recognition that partakers of the Lord's Supper should conduct themselves as persons reconciled to one another by not living at variance with their neighbors.[89] The second or third century text, *Didascalia Apostolorum*, calls people to a life marked by respectfulness and care toward others—for the bishop, the deacon, the deaconesses, presbyters, and also widows and orphans.[90]

Developing their theologies in response to the religious and social situations they faced, many early church leaders mentioned some of the socio-ethical implications of true eucharistic worship of the triune God. They recognized that a life marked by solidarity with people in need is consistent with eucharistic worship. Although it may be said that distinct features characterized each of them in their understanding of the Lord's Supper, the fathers were of one mind on this principle.

Early witnesses to the caring ministry required of Christians include Ignatius of Antioch, Justin Martyr, Clement of Alexandria, and Cyprian of Carthage. Early in the second century, Ignatius interpreted the Eucharist as an extension of Christ's incarnation, which joined the believer to Christ in the same way the Son is joined to the Father.[91] Ignatius encouraged the church to take careful note of the one cup of Jesus' blood that is shared in the Eucharist. This cup, he said, makes the believers one.[92] Ignatius taught that discernment of the presence of Christ in the Eucharist implies loving "concern for widows or orphans, for the oppressed, for those in prison or released, for the hungry or the thirsty,"[93] for widows and enslaved persons.[94]

Meanwhile Justin Martyr, perhaps reflecting practice in mid-second century Rome, observed that worshippers at the weekly Sunday Eucharist contributed to a collection that was "deposited with the president, who succours the orphans and widows, and those who, through sickness or other cause, are in want, and those who are in bonds, and the strangers sojourning among us, and in a word takes care of all who are in need."[95] Justin offers a reason for the love and solidarity that Christians exhibit. As he put it, "We who hated and killed one another, and on account of their different manners would not live with men of a different tribe, now, since the coming of Christ, live familiarly with them."[96] In Justin's understanding, the Eucharist "holds the Christian community together through the dynamic power of Father, Son, and Holy Spirit."[97]

Clement of Alexandria, who kept word and sacrament in firm communion in the Eucharist, also affirmed the social significance of that meal event. Claiming that participants in the Eucharist "are [thereby] sanctified in body and soul,"[98] Clement ascribed this divinizing process to the Holy Spirit, who enables believers to gain strength to overcome their weaknesses and to live virtuously. For Clement the liturgical event was no place for luxury and greed. In his *Protrepticus*, he stresses that instead Holy Communion is an event where people gather "with a single love" and offer "a single symphony" in anticipation of the eschatological banquet.[99] The exercise of this love was not to be confined to the eucharistic event. Clement explained that "an associate is another self; just as we call those, brethren, who are regenerated by the same word. And akin to love is hospitality, being a congenial art devoted to the treatment of strangers."[100]

For his part, Cyprian, a third-century theologian from Carthage in North Africa, understood the Eucharist to be the sacrament that proclaims the participants' unity with God and with fellow Christians. It reminds them that "there is one body with which our number is joined and united."[101] In his *Epistle 62*, Cyprian celebrates the power of the Eucharist to nourish the union between believers and Christ. Not surprisingly, therefore, Cyprian elsewhere rebuked the wealthy who wished to prevent the poor from sharing in the Eucharist because they were unable to contribute to the relief of the poor![102] In his *Epistle XXXV. To the Clergy, Concerning the Care of the Poor and Strangers*, Cyprian issued a request:

> I request that you will diligently take care of the widows, and of the sick, and of all the poor. Moreover, you may supply the expenses for strangers, if any should be indigent, from my portion, which I have left with Rogatianus, our fellow-presbyter.[103]

Some of the church leaders who later acknowledged the ethical dimensions of participation in Holy Communion include John Chrysostom, the "Cappadocians"[104]—Basil of Caesarea, Gregory of Nazianzus and Gregory of Nyssa—and Jacob of Sarugh.

Fourth-century theologian John Chrysostom regarded the Eucharist as the location where the fellowship initiated at baptism is actualized. Christ unites believers to himself in the Eucharist so that nothing can come between Christ and the communicants in his body, the church.[105] As a result of their baptism and participation in the Eucharist, Chrysostom explained in his sermon on John 6:53–54, anyone who neglects a person wasting with hunger or perishing with cold attracts the same condemnation that Judas received.[106] "[I]f thou see any one in affliction, be not curious to enquire further.

His being in affliction involves a just claim to thy aid. . . . He is God's, be he heathen or be he Jew; since even if he is an unbeliever, still he needs help."[107] Here Christians are encouraged to extend their solidarity beyond the narrow confines of the visible church community.

As Rylaarsdam has stated, Chrysostom believed that Christians as "adopted children of God, animated by the Spirit in baptism, and nourished by the Eucharist "are able to live virtuously."[108] Being benevolent to the needy is "one of the most appropriate responses to the *philadelphia* of God's adaptation to us in Christ. All alms extended to the poor are done to Christ and are an acknowledgement of his love."[109]

In responding to the needs around them, the Cappadocians complemented their writings with ministries they developed for relief of the needs of the poor. Basil of Caesarea emphatically asserts that communicants receive Christ in the Eucharist and so can participate deeply in the life of God. This implies continuity between corporate worship and the daily life of the Christian community. Basil believed the Eucharist was not a proper place for the rich to present offerings if they were treating their neighbors unjustly. His many entreaties on behalf of the poor are well known.[110] The rich, he said, should not ignore the plight of their brothers or sisters, allowing the grain to rot in their barns while refusing to feed those who are starving, or in any way ignore the oppressed![111] They should strive at "becoming honorable and glorious in [their] expenditure for the needy and not put off showing mercy." Basil states that failure to help people in need is a sign of injustice.[112]

Still in the fourth century, Gregory of Nazianzus emphasized that the Eucharist provides "medicine" that can heal both body and soul[113] and so is for those who were "desirous of true life."[114] Through "the grace of the Word sanctified," communicants in the body and blood of Christ are transformed as "God plants himself . . . in all believers by means of that Flesh, which derives its substance from both wine and bread."[115] This transformation must find expression in daily life. One sign of this change is "the most excellent form" of the virtue of love consisting in "love of the poor and compassion and sympathy for our own flesh."[116] Gregory asserted that if Christians imitated the justice of God, no one would be poor.[117]

Gregory of Nyssa placed emphasis on the way in which worshippers participate in the divine life when they receive the body and blood of Christ in the Eucharist.[118] Gregory claimed that those who receive Holy Communion have their bodies altered and changed[119] in such a way that if they hate the poor, they should "blush with shame" because they reveal the extent to which they have not experienced the restoration of the divine image in them.[120]

Another of the church leaders who grasped the link between the Eucharist and the moral dimensions of the life of the Christian community is sixth-century Syriac poet-theologian Jacob of Serugh. Jacob, who was described as "flute of the Holy Spirit and as harp of the Orthodox Church,"[121] believed that "life springs from the Service of the house of God" where members of the church are "fattened by the Table full of life."[122] Jacob was convinced that

> He with whom the Creation is full, and cannot contain Him, is knocking to enter your house in the person of the despised and the insignificant. . . . He whom the cherubim convey on their backs with trembling lies smitten on the bed of sickness, along with the sick. . . . You will find Him . . . with the sick, with those in distress, with those who mourn, with the needy, with the hungered, the buffeted and afflicted. . . . For the poor person who has stood at your door is God Himself. . . . In a lowly and despised guise, He has come to visit you, so that when you fill His belly, you will find the Bread of Life.[123]

Other examples could be cited of thinkers in the church who, during the early centuries of the church's life, attested to the social implications of Holy Communion.[124] During the twentieth century several theologians, especially from the Global South, have emphasized that the social justice implications of the Lord's Supper are not to be understood merely in terms of works of mercy and compassion. Latin American theologian Gustavo Guttiérez[125] has shown that the Eucharist, which is rooted in the Jewish Passover, is inseparably linked with liberation and covenant—the liberation that God makes possible and the covenantal relationship that God offers to the church.[126] Recalling God's own self-giving for the sake of creation, the Eucharist creates a human solidarity through joyful participation in a shared meal that the church wishes to share with others. It fashions a *koinonia* that is inhospitable to injustice and exploitation.

Gutiérrez believes the Eucharist requires a rather more radical response to poverty than mere charity. He emphatically asserts that "without a real commitment against exploitation and alienation and for a society of solidarity and justice, the eucharistic celebration is an empty action, lacking any genuine endorsement by those who participate in it."[127]

Gutiérrez's understanding of the relation of the Eucharist and justice is shared by theologians both within and outside of Latin America. One example is Sri Lankan theologian Tissa Balasuriya, who mines the treasure of biblical literature to show the rich resources available to inform an understanding "of the Eucharist in relation to the life of human beings today."[128]

Balasuriya explains that, for Jesus, "the Eucharist was essentially *action oriented*. . . . It signified his irrevocable contestation of the religious leaders of his people and the narrowness of their message. . . . It was a prelude to his agony, the preparation for his betrayal by one who drank the cup with him. The Eucharist was also to be the bond of the new community he was establishing in his new spirit."[129] The Lord's Supper offers "spiritual food" insofar as it leads to greater love, self-unity, and communion among persons and groups. This loving communion grounds "effective action for justice."[130]

When applied to the problems of the contemporary world, the subversive potential of Holy Communion looms large. Participants in the Eucharist are inspired to expose the fundamental causes of poverty, the negative consequences of economic globalization, and the many ways in which the oppression of people is fostered and perpetuated today. Christians who understand the social justice implications of Holy Communion are likely to offer a scathing critique of forces that manifest disregard for the dignity of every human being and promote causes leading to the exclusion and marginalization of people. The Eucharist inspires communicants to work against a wide range of evils, including "arms production, selfish profit maximization, ostentatious waste, and land-grabbing."[131] The reason for this is that, beyond the mere summons to love those who share in the fellowship of the church, the Lord's Supper, with its eschatological dimension, looks forward to the day when the will of God for the salvation of the world is consummated.[132]

The redemption of the entire human family and the whole of creation is within the purview of those who discern the significance of the anamnesis of the death and resurrection of Jesus. At the Lord's Table, believers are confirmed in their identity and nourished for its perpetuation. They leave the Table to love and serve those for whom Jesus offered his life at Calvary. Empowered by the Holy Spirit, the church engages in evangelical witness, making Christ known by word and deed, through service and witness. Not surprisingly, under the rubric "Hungering for Justice," British Baptists offer as one alternative pattern for the celebration of Holy Communion a service which ends with this prayer: "From the security of what we know/to the adventure of what you will reveal/Jesus now lead us. To fashion the fabric of the world/until it resembles the shape of your kingdom/Jesus now lead us."[133]

Conclusion

The meaning of Holy Communion as a community-defining and solidarity-conferring meal and the implication of the Lord's Supper for the life and witness of the church imply that Christians need to deconstruct their understanding of race and ethnicity in order to enable the acknowledgment of their common bond in Christ Jesus.[134] As von Allmen has said:

> The Eucharistic Christ-Church communion implies the brotherly communion of the members of Christ with one another . . . and this logic is not accidental or marginal. It is absolutely fundamental that this Christ-Church communion can be challenged when this communion is not expressed in terms of fraternal communion of all those joined to Christ by the Supper.[135]

Beyond this, as Gutierrez and others have shown, the eucharistic meal has implications for the church's prophetic social witness. All human beings, and the multiple dimensions of their existence, are in the church's legitimate sphere of concern. The unity of the church that shares Holy Communion has significant implications for the unity of humankind. It is a sign and instrument for that unity of human beings that God intends.

Participation in the Lord's Supper has ethical and missional implications. These include the imperative of not indiscriminately placing people into socially defined racial and ethnic groups and making judgments on them solely on this basis. This is especially indefensible in the light of the fact that people are not imprisoned in a single identity; they simultaneously have other identities as well. Furthermore, these identities are fluid and changing. The failure to see people in the rich complexity of their plural identities leads to the erection in the human community of boundary walls that are products of insensitivity and naiveté. The perpetual danger of socially constructed identities sometimes becoming almost impervious boundary markers between people becomes clearer when we consider them in the perspective of Holy Communion.

If our churches welcome and celebrate segregation based on ethnicity, this will cause attendance at their services of Holy Communion to reflect the ethnic boundary markers they create and maintain. This pattern of church attendance may be regarded as a sure sign of failure to understand how commensality not only reflects but also shapes our oneness in Christ. Ethnic apartheid has no rightful place in the Lord's Supper where Christians celebrate the existence and the continuing renewal of their communion with each other and their common mission to the world.[136]

As church members grow in grace and in the knowledge of Christ, they should increasingly overcome whatever contradicts or undermines their common partaking in their significant community meal event. This should lead them to conduct themselves in the light of T. B. Maston's reminder:

> [C]hurches that preach an all-inclusive gospel, that have said that all men are created in the image of God, that Christ died for all, that all can come to Christ through faith, that God is no respecter of persons, and that all men are of equal worth and dignity in the sight of God and should be in the sight of men . . . will be judged by the world on the basis of what they preach.[137]

Churches in ethnically diverse communities need to consider whether they can claim to celebrate the Lord's Supper with integrity when they welcome as congregants only those who are segregated on the basis of their ethnicity.

Recognizing the eschatological dimensions of the Lord's Supper, acknowledging the relationship between the memorial of Christ and the washing of the disciples' feet, and understanding the profile of the mission of the church as portrayed in Scripture, Christians should joyfully affirm without mental reservation that participation in Holy Communion commits believers to:

reconciliation and sharing among all those regarded as brothers and sisters in the one family of God and is a constant challenge in the search for appropriate relationships in social, economic and political life (cf. Mt 5:23ff; 1 Cor 10:14; 1 Cor 11:20–22). Because the Lord's Supper is the Sacrament that builds up community, all kinds of injustice, racism, estrangement, and lack of freedom are radically challenged when we share in the body and blood of Christ. Through Holy Communion, the all-renewing grace of God penetrates the human personality and restores human dignity. The Eucharist therefore obliges us to participate actively in the ongoing restoration of the world's situation and the human condition. God's judgement demands that our behaviour be consistent with the reconciling presence of God in human history.[138]

Christians will also affirm that one aspect of the vocation of the church that celebrates the Eucharist is "prophetic [and public] denunciation of every dehumanizing situation that is contrary to brotherhood, justice and liberty." They are not content with simply pointing out—and attending to—some of the consequences of injustice.[139] Their witness also addresses the fundamental causes of unjust situations.

In the perspective of the concerns raised in this chapter, Holy Communion—the depths of whose riches language can hardly plumb—should be for all Christians a sacred meal event that is a celebration of grace, a banquet of love, a festival of solidarity, and a commission to witness and service in the name of the God of love and justice. Through the Lord's Supper, God forms and shapes God's people for that unity which discourses of race and ethnicity should not be allowed to undermine or destroy. The unity God confers and commands is strong enough to overcome every form of separation that is founded on the conceptual constructions of race and ethnicity that many people seek to reify and honor.

CHAPTER 4

Avoiding Fragmentation
Human Identity and Caribbean Theology

[The Caribbean people] are generally driven by a relentless
faith in the proposition that the Caribbean belongs
to God, and that it is through faith in the God of
Jesus, expressed in radically affirming and culturally
regenerative ways, that their own spirituality will sustain
their erstwhile fragile structures of existence.

Kortright Davis[1]

The church must maintain Christian principles and point
out where the existing social order is in conflict with
them. Furthermore, it must challenge Christian citizens
to act in the spirit of Christ for the welfare of all.

Edmund Davis[2]

Our theology has to be contextual—a theology made in
the Caribbean and for the Caribbean; a "decolonization"
theology . . . which upholds the different Caribbean cultures.

Adolfo Ham[3]

One of the tasks of the church in a given culture is to contribute
to the flowering of that culture. . . . It is therefore the
reponsibility of the church to work towards genuine community,

in which each ethnic group remains faithful to its dynamic and changing identity and yet is enriched by and enriches others.

WCC *Faith and Order paper*[4]

Starting with certain convictions concerning how the incarnation grounds human identity and value, Caribbean theologians have presented African-Caribbean ethnicity as a basis on which all Caribbean people can engage in responsible theologizing. In the process, the multiple ethnic identities of the people of the region are rendered invisible, and the rich culture and history from which the theological project in the region should emerge is compromised. When the African-centered Caribbean identity becomes the norm, it ends up marginalizing many significant sectors of the Caribbean population. Furthermore, the failure to take into consideration the prevailing gendered constructions of Caribbean identity further limits the possibilities for a truly inclusive Caribbean Theology.

The incarnation can be understood as affirming the vital truth that God identifies with human beings in the specificity of their multiple cultures.[5] Cultures are rightly described as the loci of God's self-revelation to human beings[6] and so can host and reflect patterns of relationships that are consistent with the human solidarity God intends. Yet cultures have a propensity to be disordered, thereby accommodating and justifying such evils as unjust discrimination and oppression. Sometimes these features are based on the way a theologian understands the ethnicity of the people who mark the landscape where the theological project is being undertaken.

The option to affirm a constructivist view of ethnicity does not imply, when this concept is used within the theological realm, a surrender to a docetic Christology. As regards his humanity, Jesus was indeed a real person who appeared in a real cultural situation at a particular time in history. However, comprehension of the humanity of this God-human being will not be aided by perceiving Jesus merely within the limits of a narrowly conceived ethnicity. The one who appeared in the flesh was the Second Adam who offers us God's own revelation of what it means to be a human being. To speak about Jesus as Emmanuel and to adopt an incarnational theological approach is not to propose that Jesus of Nazareth is replicated in each person. An incarnational approach is intended instead to reflect the value the Triune God places on human beings in the many and varied cultural settings they inhabit.

Theologians in the Caribbean proffer the existence of a link between the Incarnation and the vitality of culture, ethnicity, and human identity. They make this claim while disavowing the "Christ of culture" stance depicted in the Niebuhrian paradigm as an acceptable approach to resolving the problem of the relation of Christian faith and civilization.[7] Among Caribbean theologians, William Watty has been outstanding in navigating the Caribbean Theology ship through rough waters to a safe harbor by affirming culture without exalting it to a level it does not deserve.[8]

From the very beginning, the idea of the Incarnation has been central to the Caribbean Theology project. Yet, as in the case of the use of the *imago dei* concept in Caribbean Theology, no exact formulation of the boundaries of the precise meaning of the Incarnation is offered. What seems clear is that the idea is confined to the appearing, life, and witness of God in Jesus Christ. It does not extend to the idea of God's embodiment in the world so that the world may be deemed in some sense "the body of God."[9] Nor does it reach toward the even broader notion of "deep incarnation"—the idea that God is present in all that exists,[10] thus broadening out the idea of Incarnation beyond anthropocentric to biocentric and even cosmocentric dimensions.[11]

Caribbean theologians claim that the Incarnation, understood as a sign of divine approbation of the integrity of diverse human cultures and ethnicities, has positive and affirming implications for people in their cultural context. As Garnett Roper has stated:

> The incarnation of Jesus Christ weaves a constant thread through Caribbean Theology. Jesus is incarnate in the poor man, the cane cutter, the enslaved, the indentured labourer and the martyr who is killed for taking a stand for justice and righteousness. The incarnation—life, ministry-death and resurrection [of Jesus]— are taken together as a complex of events in solidarity with the oppressed.[12]

Early in the development of Caribbean Theology, Samuel Carter, former chair of the Caribbean Conference of Churches, saw the fundamental role played by the theme of the Incarnation in the emerging theology:

> Jesus, though born in Bethlehem, is not a Middle Easterner, nor is he a European or an African. His incarnation is more than a past historical event. "The Word was made flesh and dwelt among us." Emmanuel—God with us—is incarnate, as well, in this rapidly developing Caribbean world of ours, and it is in discovering Him that we will finally discover to the full our own Caribbean identity.[13]

According to Carter, the desire for increased "contact, fellowship, ecumenical cooperation and [common] Christian witness" by Caribbean churches was expressed at a Caribbean Consultation on Development sponsored by the Caribbean Conference of Churches. Carter asserts that "if common Christian action is necessary for the development, social justice and the liberation of [Caribbean] people, even more necessary is the deep thought and theological reflection which enable the Caribbean man to find his true self."[14] Clifford Payne adds, with confident triumphalism, that "only a Caribbean Christ can address the deepest needs of the Caribbean people."[15]

The main figures in the early development of Caribbean Theology include Idris Hamid, William Watty, Ashley Smith, and Kortright Davis. All of these theologians from the Caribbean invoked the idea of the Incarnation as a strategy to bolster the self-worth and self-confidence of a people emerging from the bowels of colonization, exploitation, and enslavement, who now taste the freedom triggered by emancipation from slavery, the end of the system of indentured labor, and the attainment of nationhood.

Idris Hamid may be called the founding father of the movement because he was the person who, in 1971, raised the fundamental issue that was to shape the discussion on Caribbean Theology.

> God is really foreign to us. In the religious imagination of our people, he is a benign white foreigner—"an expatriate." Even the categories of our religious experiences are imports which do not reflect our cultural and native experiences. We experience God as an outsider in the bad sense of that encounter. He is not the God in our history and of our destiny. He has not been the God for us, but against us.[16]

In a move that was to lead to the harvesting of the significant idea of Incarnation for the development of Caribbean Theology, Hamid added that God "was present more in the canefields than in the cathedrals, more in the baracoons than in the basilicas." He called for theological exploration "to uncover the ways in which this God was understood and experienced" by the people. Hamid asserted God's self-offering to Caribbean people. According to Hamid, the mission of God through Jesus Christ was to give expression to God's love and irrevocable commitment to humankind, to offer a sign of God's involvement in the justice issues that people face, and "to make all things new"—that is, to open the door for new persons and new communities to emerge to the praise and glory of God.[17]

Two years after Hamid's seminal work calling for new perspectives in a theology that resonates with the experience of the people of the Caribbean, a number of Caribbean theologians gathered at two conferences on "Creative Theological Reflection." The presentations made at these conferences, which took place in Jamaica and in Trinidad and Tobago in 1973, were published that same year in *Troubling the Waters: A Collection of Papers and Responses*.[18] These papers show how concern for the development of a Caribbean Christology focused on the important function of location, history, and culture in the formation of a people's identity.

In calling for the decolonization of theology in the Caribbean, William Watty averred: "A parochial Europe-centric view of history is as spurious as it is unbiblical. . . . It is . . . possible and legitimate for the peoples of the Caribbean to understand their history theologically."[19] In this perspective, Watty rejected the idea that what awaited the emancipated Caribbean people was "degeneration, deterioration, degradation and death."[20] He noted that some people in the region had "landed themselves in a quagmire of self-depreciation"[21] and perceived in the Incarnation a way of invalidating the negative vision of the minimal possibilities that Caribbean people were deemed capable of achieving.

> If "the Word became flesh" means anything, it means that the character of Christ as an historical being must be taken seriously. There is a particularity about his person which is integral to understanding who he was. He was not a man in general . . . but a man of a particular time, beset by the limitation of a particular culture.[22]
>
> The incarnation . . . means that the same Christ that is strange to all cultures can be identified within each culture. He can be particularised in each cultural milieu. The flesh which the Word assumed was not merely Jewish flesh, but human flesh. . . . The Word dwelt among us—and that "us" means *us*.[23]

> The incarnation of Christ in our culture [calls people] to recognise the reality and concreteness of our particular and unique context and to discover how the Word is made flesh among us and [is] rejected by us. For the Christ of culture is a strange Christ. . . . As the Christ has to be rediscovered in every age, so he must be uniquely identified in every place.[24]

The principle of incarnation underlies Ashley Smith's emphatic assertion that the Caribbean church needs to be formed in, and reflect, its cultural context.[25] Smith argues that, for churches in former colonies to understand their true identity, the people of God need to learn "to perceive themselves as children [of God] with full rights in the household of faith rather than as wards of others who know themselves as children of God. . . . To be free to make its own history, a people must make the decision to end its tutelage so that it may be able to determine its own future."[26]

For the resolution of what he perceived as an identity conflict in the Caribbean church in the 1980s, Smith urged the church to "recognize its own captivity to a demonic mis-definition," to accept its authenticity and focus on the special way the church is called to fulfill the mission of God in its particular context.[27] Smith justifies both the project of creating Caribbean Theology and the discernment of the missional priorities the church should adopt[28] on the basis of the need for people to theologize according their experience in their social context and on the basis of the state of their consciousness.[29]

Kortright Davis, another major figure in the emergence of Caribbean Theology, has emphasized that the search for theological paths in the Caribbean will "recognize the unmistakable and continuing acknowledgement of an assurance of the presence of God among Caribbean people."[30] Describing the world as "a continuing sign of God's presence in the community of men,"[31] Davis attaches an "emancipatory" focus to his Caribbean Christology. He describes Jesus as "the champion of the poor, the outcasts, the weak and the helpless; he came into close contact with men and women in their broken state, and something always happened."[32] Furthermore, Davis interprets Jesus Christ as

> a historical event in the daily experiences of Caribbean people effecting the continuity of that creative relationship between God and man. The world is the community of God's continuing creative activity, in which his Spirit identifies himself with the man of faith as he attempts to live as a being-in-community.[33]

Locating his Christology within a self-evident trinitarian framework, Davis relates Jesus' "illegitimate" birth and his encounters with oppressed people, structures, and situations to the situation of Caribbean people for whom, he asserts, "the story of the Gospel is the story of the achievement of Jesus who, although he was unique, was so much like them in many respects."[34]

Davis employs the emancipation motif, which is suggested by the story of the Israelites' exodus from Egypt,[35] in evincing for the people of the Caribbean a positive sense of what they are as a people created and redeemed by God. He does this in an effort to fashion a positive vision of what Caribbean people can become in the light of God's work among them. He works out this Caribbean "emancipatory" theology in the context of a Caribbean that has been described as a meeting place of many ethnicities, religions, and cultures. It is a place where "Latin and Anglo, native Carib, African black, French and English white races (i.e., ethnicities) and cultures meet. "In a religious melting pot, Protestant and Catholic Christian, Afro-Caribbean, Hindu, and secularist faiths, intertwine, cross-pollinate, and go their ways, separate yet together, in the divine milieu." Yet, in their common quest for human freedom—its "pursuit, proclamation, and practice"—Davis locates his "emancipatory" focus that he considers central to Caribbean Theology.[36]

Other Caribbean theologians, including Lewin Williams, Burchell Taylor, and Garnet Roper, have also recognized the significant role that Christology plays in Caribbean Theology. Lewin Williams regards Christology as central to the Caribbean Theology project, which is concerned to "express the Christ reality within the Caribbean context."[37] As Williams asserts, "Caribbean Theology decides what the Caribbean Christ looks like and how the locus of liberating power, through the transcendence made available by the Incarnation, is transferred to the Caribbean context"[38] Williams claims as a significant feature of Caribbean Theology its concern to convert the Christ who was introduced to the region as an "inaccessible infiltrator" into the Christ who is "the oppressed one who, by the resurrection, liberates the oppressed ones."[39]

For his part, Burchell Taylor characterizes as the "Babylonish Captivity of the Church in the Caribbean" the failure to take the Incarnation and human liberation seriously. This failure, he says, results in the church's "captivity by complicity with the status quo," "captivity by imitation," and "theological captivity."[40] Taylor suggests that a prophetic vision of the church's cultural context and the possibility to transform it will help liberate the church to be "the collective Christian presence" in the region.[41]

Meanwhile Garnet Roper, who sees "an antecedent form of Caribbean Theology in the history of resistance by the oppressed [enslaved] people of the Caribbean,"[42] regards Caribbean Theology as public theology in the sense that its "*locus theologicus* . . . is the Caribbean itself—its origin, its history and its struggle for justice, equality and identity."[43] In this perspective, Caribbean Theology accepts "the public square and the public domain not mainly as a domain of witness, but as a sphere of the life and influence of the church." The church takes on the role of "public chaplain."[44]

Roper cites entrenched and reinforced self-doubt, the history of creolization, persistent poverty, and its location in the "shadow of empire" as fundamental to an understanding of the problem of identity in the Caribbean. He suggests that Caribbean Theology has responded to the context in which it arises partly by its orientation around

> the idea of God as Father, Son, and Holy Spirit and Lord of history . . . and the idea of Jesus incarnate in the poor, embodying the love of God, vanquishing the powers through his cross and saving by his blood and resurrection.[45]

While lamenting the absence of a comprehensive Christology in Caribbean Theology, Roper applauds Lewin Williams' effort to interpret Liberation Theology's interrogation of the traditional theories of atonement.[46] He also applauds the "strong apocalyptic overtones" in Caribbean Theology and understands these as a sign of the conviction that Jesus "confronts, unmasks and vanquishes principalities and powers." Roper anticipates the renewal of a wholesome personal identity within a social complex that has shed its idolatry, rejected values deemed false, and adopted a holistic approach that is grounded in unwavering confidence in the manifestation of divine presence in the Caribbean.

Caribbean Theology's insistence on the presence of Jesus as Immanuel, and thus its tendency to interpret Caribbean history in an incarnational way, is in the service of locating contextually the concern for a theological anthropology and an understanding of discipleship deemed appropriate to the needs of Caribbean people.

Yet the appropriation of the mystery of the Incarnation to a Caribbean that is perceived primarily through the lens of an African-centric focus reveals the danger of constructing a contextual theology which does not reflect a full appreciation of the complex ethnicities in a region.

Ethnicity, Religion, and Caribbean Theology

From time to time, Caribbean theologians have insisted on taking seriously the Caribbean—its history, cultures, and people—as the context in which the summons is issued to Christian discipleship and mission. However, from as early as the 1970s, concern has been expressed over Caribbean Theology's insufficient harvesting from the diverse ethnicities, cultures, and histories of the Caribbean people. To what extent does Caribbean Theology reflect awareness of the variety, complexity, and alignments of the ethnic collectivities that make up the region?

In 1973 Idris Hamid posited God's activity "through the cultural fragments that were among the oppressed" in the region.[47] Patrick Anthony underlined the need to investigate local folk culture to discern this. He commented on God's presence and work among the Ciboney, Caribs, and Arawaks in St. Lucia and claimed that God's ongoing work was discernible in the life and cultural traditions of the people who were often overlooked.[48]

Kortright Davis, the pioneer of Caribbean Emancipatory Theology, joined those calling for an investigation of local folk culture for signs of divine activity. Davis was convinced that, because Christ is accessible in people's history and culture, Caribbean theologians should ensure that they are cognizant of Caribbean folk wisdom and cultural history. "Indigenous religious activity," he said, was "a source of spiritual and cultural power" reflected in "proverbs . . . songs, myths, dance, movements [and] music." These are "an essential part of the matrix from which appropriate theological reflection and praxis take their departure."[49]

In 1984 George Mulrain completed a theological investigation of Haitian folk culture and criticized theologians who dismissed Haitian folk religion for exhibiting a "superiority complex." Mulrain claimed that, in so doing, these theologians deprived themselves of an opportunity to add a further dimension to their understanding of God.[50] Some ten years after Mulrain's publication, Carlton Dennis addressed aspects of this concern to examine the folk wisdom tradition of Caribbean people to discern ways in which God was at work among the people. In a dissertation presented at Drew Theological Seminary in 1995, Dennis offered a theological analysis of proverbs in use in the region and probed the meaning of this reality.[51]

If the earliest known residents in the Caribbean were the Tainos, who were virtually decimated after the invasion led by Christopher Columbus, then an authentic theology for the region should include perspectives arising from reflections on the pre-Columbian period of Caribbean history. The obligation to undertake this task is not mitigated or diminished by the fact that this indigenous segment of the contemporary Caribbean exists today in decreasing numbers.

If Caribbean theologians have been criticized for not including in the development of Caribbean Theology consideration of the culture of the indigenous people of the region, they have also been criticized for not recognizing the multiple ethnicities evident in the Caribbean. With the passage of time, concern has increased regarding the way in which diverse ethnic identities have not been given adequate attention in the development of Caribbean Theology.

Burton Sankeralli has caricatured as "Afro-Saxons" those Caribbean theologians who infuse into the creolization process what Sankeralli refers to as "a Eurocentric hegemonic spirit." He implies that the ethnic diversity of the Caribbean population has been sacrificed on the altar of the apparent assumption that the experience of the majority population in the region—the people who are of African descent—is normative for the whole Caribbean population.[52] The assignment of normativity to one ethnicity in the Caribbean represents an inadequate grasp of how God has revealed Christ in the history and culture of the region. It begins in the failure to take seriously the multiple ethnicities reflected in the Caribbean population and reduces Caribbean Theology to exclusively Black Caribbean Theology.

Caribbean theologians have been criticized for ignoring the plural religious traditions that characterize social life in the Caribbean. Idris Hamid raised the need to take into account the multiple existential forms of religious faith in the region[53] and Noel Erskine elaborated on this concern.[54] The reality of religious pluralism in the Caribbean context is now attracting attention and is contributing to the emergence of multiple Christologies within Caribbean Theology.

During more recent years, Michael Miller and Livingston Thompson have underscored the need to integrate into the construction of Caribbean Theology considerations related to the presence of multiple religious traditions in the region. This, they argue, is critical to the integrity of the Caribbean Theology project.[55]

Miller is concerned that exponents of Caribbean Theology ignore the approaches and perspectives of adherents from other religions who also reside in their context. Labeling the approach adopted in Caribbean Theology imperialist, oppressive, insular, protectionist, and arrogant,[56] Miller advances a case for Caribbean Theology to honor "otherness" in its rich variety if it is to be authentically Caribbean.

Caribbean Theology, Miller states, should not privilege the Christian perspective, but instead regard it as "a unique religious form with its own integrity" which takes its place as "one of a number of religious elements that constitute a complex whole."[57] He applies to Caribbean Theology insights drawn from various sources, including John Hick's pluralistic hypothesis, Platonic Dialectic, and Schubert Ogden's criticism of Liberation Theology as adopting classical metaphysics. He calls Caribbean theologians "Revisionist Christians" who are guilty of "oppressive parochialism."[58]

It is unclear whether Caribbean theologians will welcome Miller's appropriation of a pluralistic and dialectical approach to theological engagement in which Christians, Muslims, Hindus, and others are ready to harvest insights emerging from each other's religious perspectives. To date, the challenge Miller has put forward has not received a resounding response. Even so, there is no escaping the problem that Miller raises for those who contend for the development of a genuinely Caribbean theological identity. Livingston Thompson shares Miller's concern.

Writing from a Moravian perspective, Thompson calls for a Caribbean Theology that is truly Caribbean, authentically Christian, but not exclusivist. He suggests that Comenian and Zinzendorfian resources are available that can inform a Protestant theology of religious pluralism that can be genuinely Christian[59] without simultaneously undermining the right of people to follow other religious pathways. Thompson wants to assist Caribbean Theology to acknowledge the existence of diverse religious faiths in the region and respond to this with a "pluralism-sensitive approach" that treats the religious other with seriousness and respect.[60] He suggests that the region's theologians' positive acknowledgment of their plural religious context should be reflected in a different hermeneutical methodology employed in Caribbean Theology that yields a reconsideration of the subject of Caribbean Christology and a reconceptualization of utopia (that is, eschatology) in Caribbean Theology.[61]

In the search for a defensible methodology for a Caribbean Theology that is more fully responsive to the Caribbean social context with its multiple religious character, Thompson, like Miller, uses ideas he traces to sources from outside the Caribbean. Even if this approach does not receive a generous welcome in the Caribbean, it seems clear that Thompson's central argument is worthy of thoughtful consideration and critical reception.

Caribbean theologians regard their theological construct as one authentic interpretation of the Christian faith among others. If this is true, the neglect of insights arising from outside the region that can be applied to the subject matter and influence the methodological process of Caribbean Theology would be indefensible. From the very beginning of the Caribbean Theology project, Horace Russell sounded a word of caution regarding the consequences of failure to relate contextuality and catholicity in developing Caribbean Theology. This would represent a denial of the very principle of Incarnation that Caribbean Theology espouses.[62]

One reason why the call issued by Miller and Thompson needs serious consideration is that a strong correlation exists between ethnic identity and religious affiliation among Caribbean people. Vodoo, Rastafarianism, Santeria, and Shango are among the Creole religions found primarily among Caribbean people of African descent. Hinduism and Islam appear primarily among the descendants of indentured laborers from the Asian continent. The correlation of ethnicity, religion, and culture is highly significant for the way those undertaking the Caribbean Theology project appropriate and interpret the rich history and diverse culture of Caribbean people. The facile identification of reality in solely Afrocentric terms is indefensible and the relation of the Incarnation and multireligious and multiethnic Caribbean identity may be far more complex than some Caribbean theologians appear to assume.

This reflection on the development of Caribbean Theology demonstrates the danger posed by the close association of the church with a single ethnic group in a multiethnic society. This association is likely to reinforce one ethnic identity over other ethnic identities that exist within a community. Furthermore, the marriage of Christology to a single ethnicity in a multiethnic context may exacerbate not only divisions within the church itself, but also divisions in the society as a whole.[63] When this happens, Jesus Christ becomes the one who divides, not unites, and followers of Christ could become complicit in sowing the seeds of division rather than fostering harmonious coexistence based on the equal dignity and worth of all persons sharing a common geographical space.

Ethnicity, Gender, and Caribbean Theology

Another factor that deserves more attention from Caribbean theologians who take ethnicity seriously is the extent to which they frame their worldview in a patriarchal mode and so develop gendered understandings of faith that favor maleness. In the development of Caribbean Theology, female voices have not been adequately heard, and women's experience, based on the integrity of the female as bearer of God's image, appears to be ignored or undervalued. For this reason, a discussion of ethnicity needs to consider the fact that, whatever the composition of an ethnic group, it will necessarily include female as well as male members.[64]

The concern to overcome patriarchy in Caribbean Theology is what prompted Theresa Lowe-Ching[65] to call for that theology to incorporate a feminist approach. This, she asserted, would enable Caribbean Theology to increase its prospect of becoming "truly liberative and mature enough to have a positive impact on Caribbean existence." The adoption of a feminist approach, Lowe-Ching states, will enable Caribbean Theology to go "beyond the dualistic and oppositional structure of Western patriarchal society." Lowe-Ching is not the only Caribbean woman theologian who has expressed this concern.

In her critique of the Caribbean women's history through the lens of gender and sexuality, Althea Spencer Miller[66] detects, among other things, ways in which Christianity perpetuates "the regnant gender ideology," rooted in colonial people operating in a Eurocentric mode, to create "a form of misogyny, revealing [the churches'] unwillingness [in the pre-emancipation period] . . . to find the divine impulse in Caribbean history that departs from Eurocentric Christian doctrine and its racialized misogyny."[67]

Spencer-Miller asserts that the commodification of female slave sexuality served to foster dependency and undermine the dignity of black women vis-à-vis their white European counterparts. She notes the extent to which the policy of employing the sexuality of enslaved women for reproductive purposes compromised the church's ability to contribute significantly to the restoration of enslaved African humanity. Furthermore, on a wider Caribbean scale, Spencer Miller notes how, through the manipulation of the rules governing marriage, the churches have been complicit in entrenching "Europe's masculine domination"[68] over subjugated women.

Spencer Miller does not ignore the counter-narrative of the effort by some churches to overcome the ideologically based discourse on gender. Nor does she ignore enslaved women's action to reject and cast off the stereotypical images of them. However, she argues that, in the period before emancipation from chattel slavery, the church

> allied itself with the propagation of European ethnicity's grand narrative and the degradation of Africanisms. The African woman's body, like the European woman's, became the icon of . . . value discourses [of both missionaries and planters]. The church in its preaching and practices perpetuated and actualized this inconography. This was both moral superficiality and ideological collusion."[69]

Other Caribbean theologians, such as Hyacinth Boothe and Anna Perkins, have invited their colleagues to challenge the prevailing negative understandings and portrayals of womanhood in the region. Hyacinth Boothe claimed that "Christianity entered the Caribbean riding on the triumphalism of Western civilization and impregnated it with Western cultural assumptions [including] the perception of the inferiority of women and their exclusion from ministry."[70] This handicap, Boothe insisted, Caribbean Theology is obliged to overcome.

The case for Caribbean Theology to attend to the subject of gender finds support in the writings of Anna Perkins. In her book *Justice as Equality*,[71] Perkins evaluates the potential for transformation that lies in a certain social experiment undertaken in the region. She roots former prime minister Michael Manley's "Democratic Socialist" political strategy in Christian moral foundations. She argues that the ethical dimension of Manley's social philosophy should be examined on the ground that the philosophy aims at "making equality a central value in the political as well as the theological canons of the Jamaican people."[72] In her discussion of justice and equality in Michael Manley's Caribbean vision, she notes:

> Justice is constitutive of community and demands a special concern for those who are marginalized. A just community must seek constantly those who are excluded from its life. . . . So a preferential attention to the inclusion of persons marginalized by gender or other arbitrary criteria from full participation in the life of the community can further the good of all.[73]

Concurring on Lowe-Ching's feminist critique of Caribbean Theology,[74] Perkins asserts that a proper valuation of women is integral to the establishment of a just society.[75] She harvests insights from Delores Williams' application of the treatment of Hagar in the Hebrew Bible and insight from Galatians 4:21–5:21 to the experience of African American women.[76] She notes that Hagar is presented as the outsider *par excellence*. Hagar is a slave who has no control over her body, which belongs to her slave owner. She is sexually exploited and resists by running away. Throughout her ordeal, however, Hagar has "serious personal and salvific encounters with God." These enable Hagar and her son to survive.

Without naming Caribbean Theology specifically, Perkins notes that relegating a woman to the status of an outsider has "important resonances with some modern appropriations of the Exodus story." She adds:

[Williams] found striking similarities in the Hagar story and the story of African-American women (similarities that have echoes in the lives of Caribbean women). Hagar's heritage was as African as African-American women's (and as Caribbean as Caribbean women's).[77]

Perkins proposes that a solution to the misreading of the location of women and others disadvantaged in emerging theologies is serious attention to the hermeneutical process:

> Paying attention to the social location of the theologian will strip away any veneer of the detached, disinterested objectivism from academic discourse to reveal the complex web of presuppositions, commitments and constituencies that shape the process of reading. This requires a vulnerability, which renders interpreters accountable for their readings and the Bible accountable to the world for its lack of innocence.[78]

Those who are involved in the development of Caribbean Theology do not simply have the admonitions of Theresa Lowe-Ching and Hyacinth Boothe and the insights of Anna Perkins and other women theologians to stimulate them to further develop the project. They also have access to a vast treasure trove of published resources dealing with questions of gender and development in the region. This is primarily the result of research undertaken over the last quarter century by the University of the West Indies and its Centre, now Institute, of Gender and Development Studies (IGDS).[79]

The approach utilized by the IGDS provides a model for how to overcome some of the limitations of the methodology adopted in the Caribbean Theology project by dealing with ethnicity in a full-orbed way with eyes wide open to the Caribbean situation.

First, a sustained effort is made to insert the voices of women into the dialogue that is taking place over gender and development. Bridget Brereton laments that "women's voices have been silenced in the records of the past." As historians try "to engender history," the retrieval of these voices is deemed imperative.[80] In 1974 Lucille Mathurin-Mair started the process of rescuing Caribbean historiography from its preoccupation with maleness that leaves the role of women in Caribbean development unexplored.[81] Today the stories of women are told extensively, and representations of women are analyzed and evaluated.[82]

Second, the women engaging in the discussion of gender and development represent multiple Caribbean ethnicities.[83] This is clear from an examination of the publications by faculty, former faculty, and graduates of the IGDS program of the University of the West Indies. This inclusiveness guarantees readers' exposure to a variety of perspectives, each contributing to a rich tapestry facilitating an understanding of the diverse Caribbean situation. People of African, Asian, European, North American, and other ethnic origins and of multiple diasporic expressions of these identities participate in the discourse.

Third, the experience of women in the context of their various ethnic and religious identities is taken seriously. Rhoda Reddock once criticized "popular generalizations about Caribbean women" for failing to take into account the specific experiences of women from the multiple ethnic groups in the region. She complained that the Indian woman's experience had been relatively ignored, and she emphasized that "research into the indentureship experience of Indian women could greatly increase . . . understanding of the complex reality of the Caribbean."[84] Research into the experience of Indo-Caribbean women over the years has produced critically acclaimed texts.

Women Plantation Workers[85] is a collection of studies on the work of women in plantation societies. It was published partly to redress a deficit in published works on the plantation labor and deals rather more adequately with the role of female labor. The Caribbean component of the published discussion deals with enslaved women of African descent,[86] but it also covers indentured (contracted) Indian women in Trinidad and

Tobago[87] and in Jamaica.[88] Published works written or coordinated by Verene Shepherd, Roseanne Kanhai, and Patricia Muhammed deal with the intersection of ethnicity, religious heritage and Caribbean experience.[89]

Fourth, a considerable effort is made in the discussion of issues related to gender and development to not favor educated and wealthier women over other women. Elsa Leo-Rhynie insists that if the ultimate purpose of Women and Development Studies (WDS), as it was then called, is to improve women's lives, then the need exists for WDS to "design, develop, offer and support programmes and projects which reach nonacademic women and women whose lives are on the periphery of society." The institute, she says, should integrate research, teaching, and action.[90]

Faye Harrison probes the struggle of women in a Jamaican slum partly because she believes the struggles of Caribbean women warrant scholarly attention. She explains that these struggles "can reveal much about the part gender inequality, especially in its intersection with race [ethnicity] and class oppression, plays in colonial and postcolonial domination and in dependent forms of national development."[91] Meanwhile, extensive research undertaken by Leith Dunn has brought to light issues related, for example, to household workers and human trafficking in Jamaica.[92]

Fifth, the treatment of gender is undertaken without the writers freezing female subjects into a static mold. As Haleh Afsar has made clear:

> The static, negative identities ascribed to [women] place socioeconomic and political barriers in their path that may seem, at the first instance, to be insurmountable. The limitations that they impose mask, undermine, and devalue the rich diversities and the gamut of daily strategies that pave the paths of women across differing and fluid identities as they accommodate the needs of their daily lives. . . . [I]n the very long run, the ability of women to move

fluidly across the gamut of ascribed and adopted identities, and to function effectively in seemingly impossible circumstances, will enable them to gain appropriate recognition for their socioeconomic success and their great contributions to their states.[93]

Many writers acknowledge the fluidity and changeableness of women's multiple identities. In 1980 Gloria Joseph concluded from the research in which she participated in fifteen countries, including Guyana, Trinidad, Jamaica, Barbados and Cuba, that women suffered "to varying degrees from the oppressive nature of racial, sexual, and economic exploitation." She identified developing advocacy by "many middle and upper socioeconomic class Caribbean women" reflecting a growing desire for recognition of women's equality. However, she detected an insistence by these women that their concerns should be dealt with "from their own perspectives and historical background—not that of white women." Not only is the complex situation of women noted, but the resolve to deal with it with integrity is also recognized.[94] More recently Valerie Youssef and Patricia Muhammed, for example, have shown some of the opportunities and challenges involved in Indo-Caribbean women negotiating their identities in the Trinidadian locale.[95]

Sixth, the literature on gender and development in the Caribbean suggests a clear intention to foster women's participation in the discussion of matters under consideration. However, the involvement of men is not excluded, as exemplified by a recent publication to which Linden Lewis, David Williams, Hilary Beckles, and Keith Nurse contributed.[96] In an earlier period, Edward Kamau Brathwaite and Barry Higman also engaged in Caribbean research that deliberately included gender-based considerations.

By harvesting some of the resources provided by the IGDS and borrowing from their methodology, Caribbean theologians can correct certain deficiencies in the project they have been undertaking. IGDS resources do not focus solely on the majority ethnic population of the region or only on people traditionally aligned with the Christian religion. Nor does IGDS literature privilege educated persons at the expense of those who are socially marginalized. By drawing insights from the available IGDS literary resources, Caribbean theologians will also be able to avoid ascribed identities that are applied to women but not necessarily embraced by them. In this way they will honor women's fluid identities.

If Caribbean Theology is to focus its concern for Caribbean identity around the Incarnation and do so with integrity, it needs to take the Caribbean context into full consideration, noting the multiethnic, multireligious, multicultural aspects. In addition, it must eschew a mono-gendered approach that is unmindful of the ravages of patriarchy. As Ofelia Ortego has observed, the interdependence of women and men and the inseparability of their liberation demand attentiveness to the feminist agenda in the Caribbean.[97]

In the perspective of a Eucharistic hermeneutic, the task of developing a responsible and authentic Caribbean Theology demands attentiveness to the particularities of all Caribbean peoples, whatever their gender, ethnicity, culture, or other features. The Lord's Supper inspires a vision of wholeness, not fragmentation, and respect for wholeness leads to the creation of theological constructs that can reflect the hopes and dreams of people living in pluralistic societies.

NOTES

Acknowledgments

1 For information on the Sam Sharpe Lecture Series, see http://www.samsharpeproject.org/.
2 Information on the T. B. Maston Lecture Series is available at http://www.tbmaston.org/ and http://www.logsdonseminary.org/maston-lectures/.

Introduction

1 "Report of the General Secretary to the BWA General Council" meeting in The Netherlands. See *Baptist World Alliance Annual Gathering, July 27–August 1, 2009, Ede, Netherlands.*

Chapter 1

1 Charles Hirschman, "The Origins and Demise of the Conception of Race," *Population and Development Review* 30.2 (2004), 401 cited in *Origins of Racism in the West*, eds. Miriam Eliav-Feldon, Benjamin Isaac, and Joseph Ziegler (Cambridge: Cambridge University Press, 2009), 7–8.
2 Roger Sanjeck, "The Enduring Inequalities of Race" in *Race*, eds. Steven Gregory and Roger Sanjeck (New Brunswick: Rutgers University Press, 1996), 11.
3 *Declaration to the World by the Second Pan-African Congress of 1921*, cited in William E. B. DuBois, *The World and Africa* (New York: International Publishers, 1964 edition), 238.
4 On Marcus Garvey's life, see, for example, Rupert Lewis and Patrick Bryan, *Garvey: His Work and Impact* (Trenton, N.J.: Africa World Press, 1994); *The Philosophy and Opinions of Marcus Garvey or Africa for the Africans*, ed. Amy Garvey, 1923 (Dover, Mass.: The Majority Press, 1986) and *Selected Writings and Speeches of Marcus Garvey*, ed. Bob Blaisdell (Dover, Mass.: Dover Publications, 2004).
5 Barbara Trepagnier, *Silent Racism: How Well-Meaning White People Perpetuate the Racial Divide*, Second Edition (Boulder, Colo. and London: Paradigm Publishers, 2010), 1.

6   Delroy Reid-Salmon offers a theological interpretation of Sam Sharpe's ministry in *Burning for Freedom: A Theology of the Black Atlantic Struggle for Liberation* (Kingston: Ian Randle Publishers, 2012), which also contains a comprehensive bibliography on Sam Sharpe. See especially pp. 68–84. Other important available sources on Sharpe's work include Devon Dick, *The Cross and the Machete: Native Baptists of Jamaica—Identity, Ministry and Legacy* (Kingston: Ian Randle Publishers, 2009), 167–201; and Philip Sherlock and Hazel Bennett, *The Story of the Jamaican People* (Kingston: Ian Randle Publishers, 1998), 212–228. An informed fictional narrative on Sharpe's life appears in Fred Kennedy, *Daddy Sharpe* (Kingston: Ian Randle Publishers, 2008).

7   On five categories of slaves, see Edward Brathwaite, *The Development of Creole Society in Jamaica, 1770–1820* (Oxford: Clarendon Press, 1971), 152.

8   No unanimity exists on the number of Africans who were transported from their continent to be enslaved in the Caribbean and the Americas. Hugh Thomas, author of *The Slave Trade: The Story of the Atlantic Slave Trade, 1440–1870* (New York: Touchstone, 1997) estimates that, between 1492 and 1870, the number was about 11 million. Basil Davidson, *The African Slave Trade—A Revised and Expanded Edition* (Boston: Little, Brown and Company, 1980), 95–100; 271, calculates the number as 20 million. In *West Africa and the Atlantic Slave Trade* (Dar es Salaam: East African Publishing House, 1967), 6, Walter Rodney estimates the number at 15 million. Rodney suggests, however, that if one adds those killed in Africa "in the process of obtaining people for enslavement and those who died on board the slave ships when crossing the Atlantic Ocean, the numbers will be more likely forty to fifty million." It appears that researchers are increasingly favoring the estimate of 15 million.

9   Hilary Beckles and Verene Shepherd, *Trading Souls: Europe's Transatlantic Trade in Africans: A Bicentennial Caribbean Reflection* (Kingston: Ian Randle Publishers, 2007), xxii, cited in Cawley Bolt, "The Slave Trade and the Unholy Triangle: A Caribbean Perspective" in *Baptist Faith and Witness, Book 4*, ed., Fausto Vasconcelos (Falls Church, Va.: Baptist World Alliance, 2011), 49.

10 Aristotle, *Politics*, Book 1, Part 5, in *Social and Political Philosophy: Readings from Plato to Ghandi*, eds. John Somerville and Ronald Santoni (New York: Anchor Books, 1963), 64–65. In *Race: The History of an Idea in the West* (Washington, D.C.: The Woodrow Wilson Center Press, 1996), Ivan Hannaford claims that Aristotle's ideas on slavery have been "grossly misinterpreted and overplayed." Hannaford believes that generations of scholars have attributed to the Greeks and Roman racial attitudes they did not possess. However, Benjamin Isaac assigns the designation "proto-racism" to forms of prejudice in classical antiquity. See his *The Invention of Racism in Classical Antiquity* (Princeton: Princeton University Press, 2004) and the essay "Racism: A Rationalization of Prejudice in Greece and Rome" in *Origins of Racism in the West*, eds.

Miriam Eliav-Feldon, Benjamin Isaac, and Joseph Ziegler (Cambridge: Cambridge University Press, 2009), 32–56.

11   Henry Bleby, *Death Struggles of Slavery: Being a Narrative of Facts and Incidents Which Occurred in the British Colony During the Two Years Immediately Preceding Negro Emancipation* (London, 1853), 118, cited in Winston Lawson, *Religion and Race: African and European Roots in Conflict—A Jamaican Testament* (New York: Peter Lang, 1996), 159.

12   For a sympathetic interpretation of the racial consciousness of the missionaries in Jamaica, see Cawley Bolt, *Reluctant or Radical Revolutionaries? Evangelical Missionaries and Afro-Jamaican Character, 1834–1870* (Oxford: Regnum Books, 2013).

13   For an insightful interpretation of Sharpe's understanding of freedom, see Horace Russell, *Samuel Sharpe and the Meaning of Freedom: Reflections on a Baptist National Hero of Jamaica, Centre for Baptist History and Heritage Studies Occasional Papers Volume 5* (Oxford: Regent's Park College, 2012). Cf. Michael Miller's "realistic" libertarian understanding of freedom in *Freedom in Resistance and Creative Transformation* (Lanham: Lexington Books, 2013).

14   In *Two Jamaicas: The Role of Ideas in a Tropical Colony, 1830–1865* (New York: Atheneum, 1970), originally published by Harvard University Press in 1955, Philip Curtin adopts the name "the Baptist War" from a source he identifies as Hope Masterton Waddell, *Twenty-Nine Years in the West Indies: A Review of Missionary Work and Adventure, 1829–1858* (London, 1863), 79. In *The Story of the Jamaican People*, 212, the same revolt by enslaved people of African descent who resided in western Jamaica is referred to as "the Western Liberation Uprising of 1832."

15   Dick, *The Cross and the Machete*, 106.

16   From the *Belmore Papers*, cited in ibid., 106–107.

17   On the Castle, see William St. Clair, *The Door of No Return: The History of the Cape Coast Castle and the Atlantic Slave Trade* (New York: BlueBridge, 2007). Earlier the book appeared in the United Kingdom as *The Grand Slave Emporium* (London: Profile Books, 2006).

18   Barry Higman reports that slaveholders included enslaved persons, livestock, and machines in their inventory. *Slave Population and Economy in Jamaica, 1807–1834* (Barbados, Jamaica, Trinidad & Tobago: The University Press, 1995), 1–5. Orlando Patterson has refused to identify commodification as the defining mark of slavery, preferring loss of freedom as the primary index. See his *Slavery and Social Death: A Comparative Study* (Cambridge and London: Harvard University Press, 1982). At his death, the jury estimated Sam Sharpe's value at £16.10. See C.S. Reid, *Samuel Sharpe: From Slave to National Hero* (Kingston: Bustamante Institute of Public Affairs, 1988).

19   William Knibb, *British Parliamentary Papers*, XX (721), 246, quoted in Brathwaite, *The Development of Creole Society*, 15. Cf. *The Story of the Jamaican People*, 214.

20 See Neville Callam, "Hope: A Caribbean Perspective," *Ecumenical Review* 50, no. 2 (April 1998):137–142.
21 *Scenes in the Caribbean Sea: Being Sketches from a Missionary's Notebook* (London, 1854), 51 cited in Dick, *The Cross and the Machete*, 107.
22 Delroy Reid-Salmon, "Faith and the Gallows: The Cost of Liberation" in *Black Theology, Slavery and Contemporary Christianity*, ed. Anthony Reddie (Surrey and Vermont: Ashgate Publishing Co., 2010), 151–165.
23 See, for example, Orlando Patterson, *Slavery and Social Death* (Cambridge: Harvard University Press, 1982); Gad Heuman and Trevor Burnard, eds., *The Routledge History of Slavery* (New York: Routledge, 2011); and the four-volume history of slavery published by Cambridge University Press in 2011 and 2012 as the *Cambridge World History of Slavery*. Volume 1 deals with The Ancient Mediterranean World; Volume 2: AD 500–AD 1420; Volume 3: AD 1420–AD 1804; Volume 4: AD 1804–AD 2000.
24 For the brief discussion on the evolution of slavery in Europe, we draw extensively on the works of Richard Hart, *Slaves Who Abolished Slavery, Volume 1, Blacks in Bondage* (Kingston: Institute of Social and Economic Research, University of the West Indies, 1980), 1–20; and James Sweet, "The Iberian Roots of American Racist Thought," *William and Mary Quarterly*, 54, no. 1 (January 1997), 143—166.
25 Sweet, "The Iberian Roots," 145–146.
26 Hart, *Slaves Who Abolished Slavery*, 19.
27 See his *Freedom in the Making of Western Culture* (New York: Basic Books, 1991), 10, Patterson characterizes slavery as an extreme form of "personal domination," the enslaved being under the direct power of another. Slavery, he states, represents a form of excommunication—the enslaved being denied independent social existence—and also alienated from all rights and obligations related to their birth and their blood relations. Cf. chapter 2 of his *Slavery and Social Death*.
28 G. Gilbert to Governor. CO/137/155 (21 October 1823), 62, cited in Dave St. A. Gosse, "The Impact of the Haitian Revolution and Emancipation in Jamaica" in *Emancipation: The Lessons and the Legacy*, edited by Hopeton Dunn (Kingston: Arawak Publications, 2007), 183.
29 Hannaford, *Race: The History*, 187.
30 Sweet, "The Iberian Roots," 165.
31 Patterson, *Slavery and Social Death*, 420.
32 "Of National Characters" 3.249 (1748) cited in Hannaford, *Race: The History*, 215.
33 "Of National Characters" 3.257 in Hannaford, *Race: The History*, 216.
34 "Of National Characters" in *The Philosophical Works of David Hume*, Volume 3, eds. T. Green and T. Grose, (London: Longmans, Green, 1886), 252. Also published as David Hume, *Essays and Treatises on Several Subjects: In Two Volumes* (London and Edinburgh, 1777), vol. 1, 550.
35 If Hume was responding to James Beattie's demolition of his claim concerning people who were not white, Hume never succeeded in denying

he had espoused a racist position. For an analysis of this, see Aaron Garrett, "Hume's Revised Racism" in *Hume Studies* 26, no.1 (April 2000): 171–177.
36 *Regular Gradation of Man, and in Different Animals and Vegetables* (London: Dilly, 1799), 134, cited in Lauren, *Power and Prejudice*, 21.
37 "Occasional Discourses on the Negro Question," *Fraser's Magazine* 40 (December 1849); 670–679. http://www.efm.bris.ac.uk/het/carlyle/occasion.htm.
38 Robert Knox, *The Races of Man: A Fragment* (Philadelphia: Lea & Blanchard, 1850).
39 Knox, *The Races of Man*, 13.
40 Ibid., 14.
41 Ibid., 149.
42 Ibid., 151.
43 Ibid., 162.
44 Ibid., 163.
45 Ibid., 10. Emphasis added.
46 From the University of Uppsala's Linné on line available at: http://www.linnaeus.uu.se/online/life/8_3.html.
47 See his *Systema Naturae*, 1735. On his pseudoscientific contribution to the understanding of race, see, for example, Bloise Meneses, "Science and the Myth of Biological Race" in Robert Priest and Alvaro Nieves, eds. *This Side of Heaven: Race, Ethnicity, and the Christian Faith* (New York: Oxford University Press, 2007), 33–46.
48 In Hannaford's words, Linnaeus divided humankind into "White European, Red American, Dark Asiatic, and Black Negro." See Hannaford, *Race: The History*, 204.
49 The 1977 edition of the work is available at: www.blumenbach.info/_/De_Generis_humani_1st_Ed.html.
50 *On the Natural Varieties of Mankind*, 3rd Edition, 1795 (New York: Bergman, 1969 reprint), 269, cited in Lauren, *Power and Prejudice*, 21.
51 See Hannaford, *Race: The History*, 207–213.
52 On Jean Cuvier, popularly called Georges Cuvier, see, for example, Stephen Gould, *The Mismeasure of Man. Revised and Expanded* (New York: Norton and Co., 1996), 63–74. See also Hannaford, *Race: The History*, 256–257.
53 Hannaford, *Race: The History*, 17.
54 Ibid.
55 Harold Nicolson, *Peacemaking, 1919* (Boston: Houghton Mifflin Company, 1933), 145.
56 Even though George's grandfather and an uncle were Baptist ministers, he grew up in the Stone-Campbell movement—the tradition to which the Church of Christ (Disciples of Christ) belongs. In 1875, when he was twelve years old, George was baptized in the Penymaes Chapel, Criccieth. This former member church in the Churches of Christ joined the Baptist Union of Wales in 1939, six years before George died. Cf. David

Bebbington, "Baptist members of Parliament, 1847–1914" *Baptist Quarterly* 29 no. 1 (January 1981), 57–58. See also "Editorial Notes," *Baptist Quarterly* 16.3 (July 1955), 98.

57 Lauren, *Power and Prejudice*, 106; David Miller, *The Drafting of the Covenant* (New York: Putnam, 1928) I:116.

58 Lauren, *Power and Prejudice*, chapter 3. Thankfully, at the UN General Assembly meeting in Paris, December 1948, delegates agreed to work toward producing a *Universal Declaration of Human Rights*.

59 For the UNESCO statements on race, see *UNESCO, Four Statements on the Race Question* (Paris: UNESCO, 1969).

60 On the conceptual problem of the notion of biological race, see, for example, Dave Unander, *Shattering the Myth of Race: Genetic Realities and Biblical Truth* (Valley Forge: Judson, 2000).

61 Preamble to the Declaration. The full text was published by the United Nations in *Human Rights: A Compilation of International Instruments of the United Nations* (New York: United Nations, 1973), 22.

62 *UNESCO, Four Statements*, 50–56.

63 The Statement is available at: http://www.aaanet.org/stmts/racepp.htm. Jay Kaufman has said that "in biomedicine we may eventually recognize our biggest blunder to be the stubborn idea that socially recognized racial groupings, such as 'White,' 'Black,' and 'Asian,' have become some clinical or epidemiologic utility. The belief that continental races are genetically distinct in ways that are relevant to medicine remains prevalent in clinical research, training and practice . . . [notwithstanding the fact that] closer inspection of the putative evidence supporting such assertions reveals a more ambiguous picture." See "The Anatomy of a Medical Myth," www.raceandgenomics.ssrc.org/Kaufman/.

64 The text is accessible at http://www.un.org/WCAR/durban.pdf.

65 Statement available at http://www.iuaes.org/statement/racism.html.

66 "Science and the Myth of Biological Race" in Robert Priest and Alvaro Nieves, eds., *This Side of Heaven*, 35–37. Cf. Dave Unander, *Shattering the Myth of Race*, 43–61.

67 Ibid., 39. Cf. Carolyn Fluehr-Lobban, *Race and Racism: An Introduction* (Oxford: AltaMira Press, 2006), 104–136.

68 "Science and the Myth of Biological Race," 35. For a more extensive exposition of the myth of biological race, see Colin Kidd, *The Forging of Races: Race and Scripture in the Protestant Atlantic World, 1600–2000* (Cambridge: Cambridge University Press, 2006) and David Unander, *Shattering the Myth of Race* (Valley Forge: Judson Press, 2000).

69 Norman Goodall, ed., *The Uppsala Report 1968: Official Report of the Fourth Assembly of the World Council of Churches*, Uppsala, July 4–20, 1968 (Geneva: WCC, 1968), 241.

70 Twenty-eight such statements have been assembled in *Baptists against Racism: Reminders at the End of a Decade*, eds. Neville Callam and Julie Justus, (Falls Church, Va.: Baptist World Alliance, 2010). See also *Baptists against Racism: United in Christ for Racial Reconciliation—Addresses*

and Papers delivered at the International Summit on Baptists against Racism and Ethnic Conflict, January 8–11, 1999, Ebenezer Baptist Church, Atlanta, Georgia, Denton Lotz (McLean, Va.: Baptist World Alliance, 1999).

71 Noel Erskine, *Decolonizing Theology: A Caribbean Perspective* (Maryknoll, N.Y.: Orbis Books, 1981), 119. In a recent paper, "Prophetic of Freedom Soon Come: Reflections on Sam Sharpe, Religion, Freedom and Jamaica at Fifty," Jamaican theologian Anna Kasafi Perkins emphasized the importance of "enfleshing in social life" Sam Sharpe's "religious ideal of freedom." The paper was delivered at the Sam Sharpe Conference in Kingston on December 1, 2012.

72 Dwight Hopkins, *Down, Up and Over: Slave Religion and Black Theology* (Minneapolis: Fortress Press, 2000), 239.

73 Ibid.

74 Ibid., 240–241.

75 *South African Government Gazette*, 02/02/1996. On *Ubuntu*, see, for example, Desmond Tutu, *No Future without Forgiveness* (New York: Random House, 1999); Joe Teffo, *The Concept of Ubuntu as a Cohesive Moral Value* (Pretoria: Ubuntu School of Philosophy, 1994); Joe Teffo, *Towards a Conceptualization of Ubuntu* (Pretoria: Ubuntu School of Philosophy, 1994); W. J. Ndaba, *Ubuntu in Comparison to Western Philosophies* (Pretoria: Ubuntu School of Philosophy, 1994); Attie Van Niekerk, *Ubuntu and Religion* (Pretoria: Ubuntu School of Philosophy, 1994); Wm. Van Binsbergen, "*Ubuntu* and the Globalisation of Southern African Thought and Society;" *Quest: An African Journal of Philosophy* XV (1–2), 2001, 53–89; and Michael Battle, *Reconciliation: The Ubuntu Theology of Desmond Tutu* (Cleveland: Pilgrim Press, 1997).

76 Any criticism that seeks to undermine the rightness of appropriating the concept of *Ubuntu* in Christian theology is also applicable to the use of the concept of *koinonia*. Both terms originated in cultural and philosophical contexts that were not expressly Christian and both Greek and South African cultural milieux may be said to enjoy equivalent intrinsic value.

77 See Paul Hiebert, "Western Images of Others and Otherness" in Robert Priest and Alvaro Nieves, eds., *This Side of Heaven*, 97–110.

78 *Silent Racism: How Well-Meaning White People Perpetuate the Racial Divide*, Expanded Edition (Boulder, Colo.: Paradigm Publishers, 2010).

79 See Charles Mills, *The Racial Contract* (Ithaca, N.Y.: Cornell University, 1997).

80 *The Church in the Power of the Holy Spirit: A Contribution to Messianic Ecclesiology* (San Francisco: HarperCollins, 1975), 291–294.

81 Dwight Hopkins, *Being Human: Race, Culture, and Religion* (Minneapolis: Fortress Press, 2005), 161.

82 On this, see, for example: David Goldenberg, *The Curse of Ham: Race and Slavery in Early Judaism, Christianity and Islam* (Princeton, N.J.: Princeton University Press, 2003); Jennifer Glaney, *Slavery in Early*

Christianity (Minneapolis: Fortress Press, 2006); and Emanuel McCall, *When God's Children Get Together: A Memoir of Race* (Macon, Ga.: Mercer University Press, 2007). Careful note needs to be taken of what distinguished international lawyer Hugo Grotius has stated: "By the law of nature, in its primeval state, apart from human institutions and customs, no men can be slaves; and it is in this sense that legal writers maintain the opinion that slavery is repugnant to nature. Yet, in a former part of this treatise, it was shewn that there is nothing repugnant to natural justice, in deriving the origin of servitude from human actions, whether founded upon compact or crime." *De jure belli et pacis.* See Book 2, chapter 5 and Book 3, chapter 7, translated by Louise Loomis and published in New York by Black in 1949.

83 O. W. Taylor, editor of the *Baptist and Reflector*, the Tennessee Baptist newspaper, argued that "the plan of God is for diversity of races to continue through earthly time and into eternity. Hence, those who try to break down or obliterate racial distinctions and bring in a mongrel race or mongrel races go contrary to the plan of God." Mark Newman, *Getting Right with God: Southern Baptists and Desegregation, 1945–1995* (Tuscaloosa, Ala.: University of Alabama Press, 2001), 50. See also Richard Furman's justification for Christians owning slaves in Lucy Ford, *Deliver Us from Evil: The Slavery Question in the Old South* (Oxford and New York: Oxford University Press, 2009), 243–244; and Emmanuel McCall, *When All God's Children Get Together: A Memoir of Race and Baptists* (Macon, Ga.: Mercer University Press, 2007).

84 Carolina Redfearn, "A Legacy of Slavery—Black with the Slaves or Mulatto with the Slavers? An English Jamaican Theological Reflection on the Trajectories of 'Mixed Race Categories'" in *Black Theology, Slavery and Contemporary Christianity*, ed. Anthony Reddie, 140.

85 J. Kameron Carter, *Race: A Theological Account* (New York: Oxford University Press, 2008), 233. Carter highlights theology's complicity in constructing the racialized world and calls for theology to adopt a new discourse.

86 The Fourth World Conference on Women, which met in Beijing in September 1995, adopted the Beijing Platform for Action, identified the intersection of gender and racial discrimination and provided groundwork for the claim that the various categories of discrimination do not necessarily affect women and men in the same way. See the *Report of the Fourth World Conference on Women, Beijing, 4–15 September 1995* (New York: United Nations, 1996). In "The Primacy of Gender in Race and Class" in *Race, Class and Gender in the Future of the Caribbean*, ed. J. Edward Greene (Mona, Kingston: Institute for Social and Economic Research, 1993), 43–73, Rhoda Reddock challenges the understanding of gender as "a primarily sociological form, as a social category" rather than as "a conceptual understanding of social reality which transforms [the] very perception of class."

87 Gustavo Gutiérrez, *Las Casas: In Search of the Poor of Jesus Christ*, trans. Robert Barr (Maryknoll, N.Y.: Orbis Books, 1993), 458.

88 This confession was drafted in 1933 by Dietrich Bonhoeffer, Georg Merz, Hermann Sasse, and others. It was an effort to confess the Christian faith in the midst of a situation which rightly called into question Christian solidarity with the Jewish people. See Eric Metaxas, *Bonhoeffer: Pastor, Martyr, Prophet* (Nashville: Thomas Nelson, 2010), 183–194.

89 John De Gruchy, *Daring, Trusting Spirit: Bonhoeffer's Friend Eberhard Bethge* (Minneapolis: Fortress Press, 2005), 9. On this, see also eds. John De Gruchy and Charles Villa-Vicencio, *Apartheid is Heresy* (Grand Rapids: William B. Eerdmans Publishing, 1983).

90 On August 10, 1872, the Pan-Orthodox Synod in Istanbul pronounced an official condemnation on "ethno-phyletism," or ecclesiological racism. It declared: "We renounce, censure and condemn racism, that is racial discrimination, ethnic feuds, hatreds and dissensions within the Church of Christ, as contrary to the teaching of the Gospel and the holy canons of our blessed fathers." Racism openly contradicts "the spirit and teaching of Christ." See http://www.incommunion.org/category/news-reports/.

91 See, for example, Neville Richardson, "Apartheid, Heresy and the Church in South Africa," *The Journal of Religious Ethics* 14, no. 1 (Spring, 1986), 1–21; Lennart Henricksson, *A Journey with a Status Confessionis: Analysis of an Apartheid-Related Conflict between the Dutch Reformed Church in South Africa and the World Alliance of Reformed Churches, 1982–1998* (Uppsala: Swedish Institute of Missionary Research, 2010); Henry Hamann, "Status Confessionis" in *A Lively Legacy: Essays in Honor of Robert Preus*, eds. Kurt E. Marquart, John R. Stephenson, and Bjarne W. Teigen (Fort Wayne, Ind.: Concordia Theological Seminary, 1985), 40 ff.; and Peter Lodberg, "Apartheid as a Church Dividing Issue," *The Ecumenical Review* 48, no. 2 (April 1996): 173–177. The notion of *status confessionis* has deep roots in the Reformation.

92 The LWF decision was made at their sixth assembly in Dar es Salaam, Tanzania, in June 1977.

93 The WARC's affirmation was issued at their General Council meeting in Ottawa, Canada, in August 1982. At their Assembly in Debrecen, Hungary, in 1997, WARC initiated a *processus confessionis* in an effort to educate the churches on how their response to issues of economic justice could trigger the declaration of a *status confessionis*.

94 See J. Deotis Roberts, *Bonhoeffer and King: Speaking Truth to Power* (Westminster: John Knox Press, 2005), 88–89. In 1956, twenty-one years before the LWF arrived at its decision, English Anglican Bishop Trevor Huddleston had declared that "racialism" in any form is an "inherent blasphemy" against the nature of God who has created human beings in God's own image. Huddleston also argued that the Calvinism espoused by the Dutch Reformed Church in South Africa "like all heresies and deviations from Catholic truth . . . is sub-Christian." See his *Naught for Your Comfort* (Garden City, N.Y.: Doubleday, 1956). It is noteworthy that, from its inaugural Assembly in Amsterdam in 1948, WCC

had declared that "anti-semitism is sin against God and man." This was the conclusion of Assembly Committee IV, which dealt with one of the four concerns of the churches identified at the assembly, namely "The Christian Approach to the Jews." This did not approximate to the ecumenical body declaring itself in *status confessionis* with regard to a serious social issue with deep moral implications, but it came close to it. See *Man's Disorder and God's Design: The Amsterdam Assembly Series* (New York: Harper & Brothers, Publishers, 1949), which contains papers delivered before the four groups at the Assembly. Section 3, which was chaired by Reinhold Niebuhr, dealt with "The Church and the Disorder of Society." See also Jeffrey Gros, "Eradicating Racism: A Central Agenda for the Faith and Order Movement" in *Ecumenical Review* 47, no. 1 (January 1995), 42–51; and Hugh McCullum, "Racism and Ethnicity" in *A History of the Ecumenical Movement, Volume 3, 1968–2000*, eds. John Briggs, Mercy Oduyoye, and George Tsetsis (Geneva: WCC Publications, 2004), 345–372. Since 2000, important developments on the racism front have taken place in WCC, including significant work by the Faith and Order Commission and the Commission on World Mission and Evangelism, and through the Central Committee. Through its official participation in the UN-sponsored World Conference against Racism, Racial Discrimination, Xenophobia and Related Intolerance in Durban, South Africa, in 2001, its sponsorship, through the Program to Combat Racism, of the Doorn Conference in Utrecht, The Netherlands, in 2009, and the 2010 Cleveland Conference on Racism Today, the World Council of Churches has displayed what appears to be a renewed effort to call attention to the fundamental theological problem that racism poses and the persistence of rampant racism despite all the efforts to overcome it.

95 Sheryl Kujawa-Holbrook tells a compelling story about how, influenced by a Jamaican, a congregation in Massachusetts worked to come to terms with its historical association with the slave trade. See her *A House of Prayer for All Peoples: Congregations Building Multiracial Community* (Bethesda: Alban Institute, 2002), 152–176.

96 See Willie Jennings, *The Christian Imagination: Theology and the Origins of Race* (New Haven & London: Yale University Press, 2010), 289–294. Jennings alleges the replacement of race with a "place and place-centered identity" that keeps "renewing with each generation of race-formed children." Rather than issuing a call for "the elimination of race," he asserts that what is needed is a new order in which boundary-defying relationships will mark the new living spaces created in a new order that hosts "different ways of life that announce invitations for joining."

Chapter 2

1 Paul Weller, "The Changing Face of Europe: The Nature and Role of Ethnic Minorities in European Societies" in *Ethnic Churches in Europe:*

A Baptist Response, ed. Peter Penner (Germany: Neufeld Verlag Schwarzenfeld, 2006), 25.
2 Ann Morning, "Ethnic Classification in Global Perspective: A Cross-National Survey of the 2000 Census Round," *Population Research and Policy Review* 27, no. 2 (2008): 264.
3 *Participating in God's Mission of Reconciliation: A Resource for Churches in Situations of Conflict*, Faith and Order Paper No. 201(Geneva: World Council of Churches), 2006, §85.
4 Ann Morning illustrates the different approaches to the matter of race adopted by the medical establishment in New York and Milan when collecting data from pregnant women who were their clients. See Morning's *The Nature of Race: How Scientists Think and Teach about Human Difference* (Berkeley, Calif.: University of California Press, 2011), 1–2; 219–220.
5 See, for example, Thomas Ericksen, *Ethnicity and Nationalism: Anthropological Perspectives, Third Edition.* (London and New York: Pluto Press, 2010), 4.
6 Ibid.
7 See, for example, Enoch Wan and Mark Vanderwerf, "A review of the literature on 'ethnicity' and 'national identity' and related missiological studies," GlobalMissiology.org "Featured Articles" April, 2009: Note 8.
8 Thomas Eriksen, *Ethnicity and Nationalism*, 4.
9 In literature written in the postmodern perspective, ethnicity is said to have "no essence or center, no underlying features or common denominator." Vide Anthony Smith, *Nationalism and Modernism* (London: Routledge, 1998), 204.
10 Cynthia Enloe, "Religion and Ethnicity" in *Ethnicity*, eds. John Hutchinson and Anthony D. Smith (Oxford and New York: Oxford University Press, 1996), 197.
11 "Ethnicity in the Social Sciences: A view and review of the literature on ethnicity" available at the following address: http://ojs.globalmissiology.org/index.php/english/article/view/194/542.
12 In Wan and Vanderwerf, "A review of the literature," the authors identify the scholarly works of D. K. Buell, M. G Brett, Nicola Denzey, A. J. Blast, J. Duhaime, P.A. Turcotte Philip Esler, Dennis Duling, David Edward Aune, John Fotopoulos, Shaye Cohen, and Eckhard J. Schnabel, for example, as signifying the increasing attention missiologists, biblical scholars, and theologians are paying to ethnicity in some of its aspects. Other theological, missiological, and biblically based books dealing with ethnicity include Curtis Paul DeYoung, *Coming Together in the 21st Century: The Bible's Message in an Age of Diversity* (Valley Forge: Judson Press, 2009) and *This Side of Heaven*, eds. Robert Priest and Alvaro Nieves (Oxford University Press, 2007).
13 Peter Penner, *Ethnic Churches in Europe*.
14 Ibid., 26–27.
15 See, for example, ibid., 17.

16 Ibid., 43.
17 "International and Multiethnic Churches" in Penner, *Ethnic Churches*, 155.
18 "Immigrant Churches in the German Baptist Union" in Penner, *Ethnic Churches*, 189.
19 Ibid., 191.
20 Carmine Bianchi, "Case Study from Italy" in Penner, *Ethnic Churches*, 211.
21 "Immigrant Churches in the German Baptist Union" in Penner, *Ethnic Churches*, 211.
22 Ibid., 212.
23 "Portugal: The Challenge of Immigration and the start of Baptist Congregations among Immigrants" in Penner, *Ethnic Churches*, 227.
24 Ibid., 230.
25 "France: Christians from Elsewhere" in Penner, *Ethnic Churches*, 231.
26 Ibid., 233.
27 "The Multi-ethnic and Ethnic Work and Strategies in the Norwegian Baptist Union Initiated in 2005: Experiences and Current Results" in Penner, *Ethnic Churches*, 221.
28 See, for example, ibid., 224.
29 In an editorial, the militant segregationist Leon Macon, 1908–1965, of *Alabama Baptist* opined: "We think it is deplorable in the sight of God that there should be any change in the difference and variety in his creation and he certainly would desire to keep our races pure." See Mark Newman, *Getting Right with God: Southern Baptists and Desegregation, 1945–1995* (Tuscaloosa, Ala.: University of Alabama Press, 2001), 50. Later, Macon slightly moderated his position when he stated in a May 3, 1956, editorial: "As for our churches, the present segregated conditions were brought about by the expressed desire and wish of our colored brethren." Any move to integrate the South's social institutions should occur gradually and not "through sudden decisions and acts," which "would cause violent repercussions." On Baptists and segregation in the southern states of the United States, see Mark Newman, "White Minority Culture in the Southern States of the USA: The Southern Baptist Example," *Politics of Identity: Migrants and Minorities in Multicultural States*, eds. Robert Hudson and Fréd Reno (New York: St. Martin's Press Inc., 2000), 83–114 and Wayne Flynt, "Baptists in Black and White: Evangelical Diversity During the Montgomery, Alabama, Bus Boycott" in *Baptist Identities: International Studies from the Seventeenth to the Twentieth Centuries*, eds. Ian Randall, Toivo Pili, and Anthony Cross (Eugene, Oreg.: Wipf & Stock Publishers, 2006), 191–198.
30 "An important time for Southern Baptists," *The Alabama Baptist*, May 19, 2011 and "The Hallmark of the Phoenix Convention," *The Alabama Baptist*, June 23, 2011. One example of concurrence with Terry's understanding of ethnicity by some Christians in the United States is found in Robert C. Crosby's article, "A New Kind of Pentecostal"

which appeared in *Christianity Today*, August 3, 2011. Crosby attempts an elucidation of the factors contributing to the increased attention to social issues in North American Pentecostalism. Among these, he lists changing demographics. Crosby claims that: "While the predominantly white U.S. Pentecostal denominations have seen their growth rates level off in recent years, non-white churches are exploding." This, he says, is especially true in the case of Hispanic congregations. He cites Samuel Rodriguez, president of the National Hispanic Christian Leadership Conference, as saying, "By the end of the 21st century, the majority of Pentecostals in North America will be non-white. [Some say this will occur as early as year 2050]. For decades American Pentecostalism has been predominantly white and rural. It will soon become primarily ethnic and urban." Crosby adds this: "Rodriguez notes that Pentecostals have traditionally held 'a vertical worldview of their faith, focusing on personal beliefs and a salvation that prepares one's soul to make the Rapture.' White Pentecostals say, 'I receive the power of God to live a holy life in order to go up in the Rapture.' Ethnic Pentecostals, on the other hand say, 'I am saved by grace, but I also receive the power of God so my family can be transformed, and so we can overcome social ills and gangs in our neighborhood.' The priorities of this [ethnic Pentecostal] community are issues of life, biblical marriage, education, sex trafficking, immigration reform, poverty alleviation—all under the canopy of the Great Commission." Crosby makes a clear distinction between "white Pentecostals" and "ethnic Pentecostals," with the clear implication that those who are white are excluded from the group tagged "ethnic."

31 The 2011 SBC meeting was to receive a report from its Executive Committee that the 2009 SBC meeting had commissioned to "study greater SBC involvement for ethnic churches and leaders." The report focused on the involvement of persons from "ethnic churches" in the life of the SBC. It is not clear that the focus on mere participation was undergirded by a deep desire for transformation of the SBC. The logic of inclusion cannot simply be assumed to include a commitment to transformation through fuller representative participation in the life of a group.

32 Perhaps some persons do not know that to identify a person as an ethnic, which is popular usage in some "immigrant countries," is actually offensive to many of those so categorized in other parts of the world. See, for example, the note added under "ethnic" in www.dictionary.com indicating that "usage referring to a person as *an ethnic* is broadly acceptable in the US, Australia and Canada, but could well cause offence in the UK and elsewhere."

33 Cf. the report that appeared in *Baptist Press*, June 15, 2011.

34 Other State convention papers reflect a diminished understanding of the relevance of Luter's ethnicity. Illinois' *Baptist Standard* 105, no. 12 (June 20, 2011) mentioned the appointment only in passing. In the lead article in Louisiana's *Baptist Message* 126, no. 13 (June 23, 2011), Joni Hannigan highlighted as a "historic measure" SBC's overwhelming

approval of an "ethnic recommendation." In his article, entitled "SBC Meeting Spotlights Diversity, Unity, Unengaged," Michael Faust reported that SBC messengers "adopted an historic report encouraging ethnic diversity" but did not mention the election of Fred Luter. The report on Luter's election was written by Barbara Denman, who did not elaborate on the historic significance of the event. Kentucky's *Western Recorder* (Vol. 185, No. 24, June 21, 2011) and also Texas' *Baptist Standard* (Vol. 123, No. 12, June 20, 2011) reproduced the *Religion News Service* report written by Adelle Banks. Banks reported that Southern Baptists "adopted a plan to boost minorities in their top leadership posts" and located this decision in the answer to "continuing reports of stagnant baptism rates and declining membership." According to Banks, "Southern Baptist leaders say half the churches started in the last decade were predominantly African-American or ethnic, and the number of churches with mostly minority membership increased from 13 per cent to 18.5 per cent between 1998 and 2008," adding, "In recent decades, the convention has passed 11 resolutions seeking 'greater ethnic participation,' including a 1995 resolution apologizing for its past defense of slavery." In the June 28, 2011, issue of *Western Recorder*, editor Todd Deaton, commenting on the SBC meeting, said: "Recognizing that our nation is changing demographically, Southern Baptists took a significant step toward becoming proactive in seeking greater diversity in leadership and more intentional about increasing participation of all ethnic identities and races. According to Deaton, SBC leaders found out that "only a few ethnicities or races are represented" on SBC boards and committees. He reported Ed Stetzer, vice president of the Research and Ministry Development Division, as saying, "We've been so Southern and so white for so long that the annual meetings look like a loaf of Wonder Bread. Our ideas of 'reaching out' are less impressive than striving to create an intentionally multicultural family that reflects the population of heaven." Deaton explained that Chris McNairy, a leader on the SBC multiethnic mobilization team, urged "ethnics and Anglos to work together in reaching all people for Christ." At the end of his article he asked, "Will Kentucky Baptists strive harder to embrace all races and ethnicities as our brothers and sisters in Christ and be willing to partner with them in serving our Savior?" An article in Mississippi's *The Baptist Record*, 135, no. 25 (June 23, 2011) described the SBC Executive Committee report on ethnic diversity as a "landmark report" and "an historic report encouraging ethnic diversity."

35 Richard Schermerhorn's *Comparative Ethnic Relations* (New York: Random House, 1970), 12.
36 Thomas Ericksen, *Ethnicity and Nationalism*, 5 & 109.
37 Hutchinson and Smith, *Ethnicity*, 6.
38 See Clifford Geertz, "The Impact of the Concept of Culture on the Concept of Man" in *New Views of the Nature of Man*, ed. John R. Platt (Chicago: University of Chicago Press, 1965) 16–29. See also Paul

Hiebert, *Anthropological Insights for Missionaries* (Grand Rapids: Baker Book House, 1985), especially 15–28.
39 Ann Morning, "Ethnic Classification," 240 and 241.
40 The cultural anthropologist, Clifford Geertz may be identified as an example of primordialists. See his *The Interpretation of Cultures* (New York: Basic Books, 1973).
41 Morning, "Ethnic Classification," 260.
42 Morning shows that ethnic enumeration has both causes and effects and she thinks that "governments that are concerned about national unity avoid the use of ethnic classification in their census enumeration process." Ibid., 264.
43 *Ethnic Groups and Boundaries* (Boston: Little, Brown and Co., 1969).
44 Anthony Smith, "Chosen Peoples" in *Ethnicity*, eds. John Hutchinson and Anthony D. Smith (Oxford: Oxford University Press, 2009), 189–197.
45 *The Ethnic Origins of Nations* (Oxford: Blackwell Publishers Ltd., 1986). In her essay, "Essentialism versus Constructivism: Time for a Rapprochement?" in *Gendered Realities: Essays in Caribbean Feminist Thought*, ed. Patricia Muhammed (Kingston: University of the West Indies Press; Mona, Jamaica; Centre for Gender and Development Studies, 2002), 3–21.
46 See Samuel Johnson, *The History of the Yorubas: From the Earliest Times to the Beginning of the British Protectorate* (London: Routledge & Kegan Paul, 1921), cf. Eriksen, *Ethnicity and Nationalism*, 112–115. Akintoye traces the origins of the Yoruba people to the Ilé-Ifẽ of what is now south western Nigeria. See his book *A History of the Yoruba People* (Dakar: Amalion, 2010). Cf. William Bascom, *The Yoruba of South Western Nigeria* (Prospect Heights: Waveland Press, Inc., 1984).
47 Philosophers like Thomas Hobbes, John Locke, Jean Jacques Rousseau, and John Rawls significantly exemplify modes of thinking about society in social contractarian terms.
48 See, for example, Anton L. Allahar, "The Politics of Ethnic Identity Construction," *Identity: An International Journal of Theory and Research* 1, no. 3 (2001): 197–208.
49 This author addressed the members of the Black and Ethnic Coalition during the May 2009 Assembly of the Baptist Union of Great Britain. I asked the gathering to consider how far their acceptance of the designation "Black and Ethnic Coalition" may actually reflect acquiescence to group disparagement that is secured through the shoring up of boundaries of exclusion. I inquired into whether the group name represented the embrace of a ghettoized group self-understanding, and I asked how the spiritual riches of the group were identified, celebrated, and shared.
50 For an excellent analysis of how the notion of the image of God has been understood throughout history, see Stanley Grenz, *The Social God and the Relational Self: A Trinitarian Theology of the Imago Dei* (Louisville: Westminster John Knox Press, 2001), 141–182.

51 *Christian Perspectives on Theological Anthropology*, Faith and Order Paper No. 199 (Geneva: World Council of Churches, 2005), §94.
52 See ibid., §75–91.
53 See Genesis 10.
54 *Participating in God's Mission of Reconciliation*, §102–107.
55 See, for example, Galatians 3:26–28.
56 Ephesians 2:13–14. Based on the teaching in the Letter to the Ephesians, Philip Turner develops an impressive portrait of God's will to unify all things in Christ and to bring them under God's reign. See his *Christian Ethics and the Church: Ecclesial Foundations for Moral Thought and Practice* (Grand Rapids: Baker Academic, 2015), 61–76.
57 My argument closely reflects the pattern of argumentation that appears in *Participating in God's Mission of Reconciliation*, §§91–101.
58 See, for example, Ezra 9–10 and Nehemiah 13:23–30.
59 See, for example, Joshua 7; 1 Samuel 15; and 1 Kings 18, 20.
60 *Participating in God's Mission of Reconciliation*, §95. The following New Testament writings distinguish between physical lineage and spiritual lineage: John 2:13; 3:5–15; Galatians 3:25–29; 4:29; and Romans 8:12–17.
61 See, for example, James Crenshaw, *A Whirlpool of Torment: Israelite Traditions of God as an Oppressive Presence* (Philadelphia: Fortress Press, 1984); James Williams, *The Bible, Violence, and the Sacred: Liberation from the Myth of Sanctioned Violence* (San Francisco: Harper Collins, 1991); Mark McEntire, *The Blood of Abel: The Violent Plot of the Hebrew Bible* (Macon, Ga.: Mercer University Press, 1999); Phyllis Trible, *Texts of Terror: Literary-Feminist Readings of Biblical Narratives* (Philadelphia: Fortress Press, 1984); and Walter Wink, *Engaging the Powers: Discernment and Resistance in a World of Domination* (Minneapolis: Fortress Press, 1992).
62 See, for example, Luke 10:25–37; John 4:9; Acts 10:34; Romans 2:11; Ephesians 6:9; Colossians 3:25; and James 2:1. Sugirtharajah names six ways of "untangling mixed messages" from "sacred narratives as inflammable sources." See R. S. Sugirtharajah, *Troublesome Texts: The Bible in Colonial and Contemporary Culture* (Sheffield: Sheffield Phoenix Press, 2008), 84–91. On interpreting the Bible in the Caribbean context, see, for example, George Mulrain, "Hermeneutics within a Caribbean Context," in *Vernacular Hermeneutics*, ed. R. S. Sugirtharajah (Sheffield: Sheffield Academic Press, 1999), 11–132; N. Samuel Murrell, "Hermeneutics and Interpretation, Part 2: Contextual Truths in Sub-Version Preaching," *Caribbean Journal of Evangelical Theology* 3 (1999): 48–64; and David Kuck, *Preaching in the Caribbean: Building Up a People for Mission* (Kingston: Faith Works Press, 2007), 66–91, 169–185.
63 For the classic text that illustrates the definition of the situation approach, see William Thomas and Florian Znaniecki, *The Polish Peasant in Europe and America*. 2 vols. Second Revised Edition (New York: Dover

Publishing Inc., 1958), published earlier by A. A. Knopf in 1927. Or see Neville Callam, *Deciding Responsibly: Moral Dimensions of Human Action* (May Pen: Grace Social Ethics Books, 1985), 42–45.

64 Frank Yamada and Leticia Guardiola-Sáenz, "Culture and Identity" in *Coming Together in the 21st Century: The Bible's Message in an Age of Diversity*, ed. Curtiss DeYoung (Valley Forge, Pa.: Judson Press, 2009), 32.

65 See Y. S. Kostylev's "The Image of a Pole in Official Soviet Texts" in *Proceedings of Ural State Pedagogical University, Linguistics*, 19 (2006), 131–147.

66 Harry Lucenay, "Preaching the Truth across Cultures," *Window: Ministry Resources from the Logsdon School of Theology*, 12, no. 1 (Spring 2009), 6.

Chapter 3

1 Andrew Packman, "Table Manners: Unexpected Grace at Communion," *The Christian Century*, January 24, 2012: 11.

2 Horton Davies, *Bread of Life and Cup of Joy: Newer Ecumenical Perspectives on the Eucharist* (Grand Rapids, Mich.: William B. Eerdmans Publishing Company, 1993), 210.

3 Edourd Boné, "The Church as Eucharistic Community and the Renewal of Human Community" in *Church, Kingdom, World: The Church as Mystery and Prophetic Sign*, Faith and Order Paper No. 130, ed. Gennadios Limouris (Geneva: World Council of Churches, 1986), 87.

4 Curtis Freeman, *Contesting Catholicity: Theology for Other Baptists* (Waco, Tex.: Baylor University Press, 2014), 324.

5 Igino Giordani, *The Social Message of the Early Church Fathers*, 1944 (Boston: Daughters of St. Paul, 1977), 298.

6 As the Faith and Order text on *One Baptism: Towards Mutual Recognition*, Faith and Order Paper No. 210, (Geneva: World Council of Churches, 2011) makes clear: "Most traditions, whether they use the term 'sacrament' or 'ordinance,' affirm that these events are both *instrumental* (in that God uses them to bring about a new reality) and *expressive* (of an already-existing reality). Some traditions emphasize the instrumental dimension, recognizing baptism as an action in which God transforms the life of the candidate as he or she is brought into the Christian community. Others emphasize the expressive dimension. They see in baptism a God-given and eloquent demonstration, with the Christian community, of the gospel and its saving power for the person who, being already a believer through his or her encounter and continuing relationship with Christ, is then baptized (§30). Those who prefer the language of sacrament often regard baptism also as an ordinance, recognizing that it is performed following Christ's command and example. Some—though not all—who prefer the term ordinance may, in fact, give

the act a sacramental meaning. These two approaches represent different starting points in understanding baptism. They are not mutually exclusive and may both be regarded as essential for understanding the full meaning of baptism (§31)." See *The Church: Towards a Common Vision*, Faith and Order Document No. 214 (Geneva: World Council of Churches, 2013), §25–27, 40–44.
7 1 Corinthians 11:20.
8 The association of Eucharist with the meal is connected to Jesus' use of *eucharistein*. This is reflected, for example, in the passage on the Last Supper in Mark 6:41 and its parallels in Matthew 14:29 and Luke 6:11; in the story of the feeding of the thousands in Mark 8:6 and Matthew 13:36; and in the story of Jesus at table with the men he met on the Emmaus road in Luke 24:30. See, for example, Horton Davies, *Bread of Life and Cup of Joy*, 17–48.
9 *Baptism, Eucharist and Ministry*, Faith and Order Paper No. 111 (Geneva: World Council of Churches, 1982), Eucharist II: 2.
10 On the church as "mystery and prophetic sign," see *Church, Kingdom, World: The Church as Mystery and Prophetic Sign*. See also *Church and World: The Unity of the Church and the Renewal of Human Community*, Faith and Order Paper No. 151 (Geneva: WCC Publications, 1990).
11 Significantly, John Calvin understood the Lord's Supper as an event that bears witness to "our growth into one body with Christ such that whatever is his may be called ours" (IV.xvii.2). See his *Institutes of the Christian Religion*, especially Book IV. xvii in *Calvin: Institutes of the Christian Religion*, ed. John T. McNeill, trans. Ford Lewis Battles, in collaboration with the editor and a committee of advisers (Philadelphia, Westminster Press, 1960), 1359–1428. On the emphasis on the social aspect of the communion in the writings of Robert Jenson, Wolfhart Pannenberg, and John Zizioulas, see Todd Murken, *Take and Eat, and Take the Consequences: How Receiving the Lord's Supper is an Action That Makes a Difference* (New York: Peter Lang, 2002), 26–33. Geoffrey Wainwright credits the modern liturgical renewal for "the increased frequency of communion and the recovery of the meal symbolism." See *Doxology: The Praise of God in Worship, Doctrine and Life—A Systematic Theology* (New York: Oxford University Press, 1980), 32.
12 *Baptism, Eucharist and Ministry*, Eucharist II. A-E.
13 It should be emphasized that the approach to the discussion of Holy Communion that is reflected in this chapter—the Eucharist as a meal event—does not imply that this is *the* exclusive way in which the Lord's Supper should be interpreted. All that the Eucharist means cannot be subsumed fully under the metaphor of an event. Nor does this writer believe that the meaning of the event can be derived wholly from either the words of the institution or on the act of partaking. On this, see Albert Schweitzer, *The Problem of the Lord's Supper*, trans. A. J. Mattill, Jr. (Macon: Mercer University Press, 1982). However, the event-centered

understanding of the meal may fruitfully be considered. It should also be noted that Holy Communion is presented here as a single service of word and table, and the aspect of the Eucharist as a community meal is regarded as fundamental to an understanding of the meaning of the whole event. [On this, see Gordon Lathrop, "The Lima Liturgy and Beyond: Moving Forward Ecumenically" in *Eucharistic Worship in Ecumenical Contexts: The Lima Liturgy—and Beyond*, eds. Thomas Best and Dagmar Heller (Geneva: WCC Publications, 1998), 24–25. For an excellent treatment of the *ordo* of Christian worship, see Lathrop's *Holy Things: A Liturgical Theology* (Minneapolis: Fortress Press, 1993)].

14 William Robertson Smith is perhaps the first anthropologist to draw the link between a shared meal and kinship. In his research into sacrificial practices among the Arabs and Israelites, he saw that the social act of participating in a shared meal "was a symbol and a confirmation of fellowship and mutual social obligations." See his *Kinship and Marriage in Early Arabia* (Cambridge, UK: Cambridge University Press, 1890), 251–293.

15 Mary Douglas, "Deciphering a Meal" in *Myth, Symbol, and Culture*, ed. Clifford Geertz (New York: Nortand and Co, 1971), 36.

16 Ibid., 44.

17 *Homo Hierarchicus: The Caste System and Its Implications*, trans. Mark Sainsbury (Chicago: University of Chicago Press, 1970). See especially chapter 6. An expanded and updated version of *Homo Hierarchicus* "with a new Preface and Postface" was published by the University of Chicago Press in 1980.

18 Dumont's essentialist understanding of caste contrasts with a constructivist understanding which developed later and is reflected in the writings of anthropologists such as Bernard Cohn, *Colonialism and Its Forms of Knowledge: The British in India* (Princeton: Princeton University Press, 1996) and Nicholas Dirks, *Castes of Mind: Colonialism and the Making of Modern India* (Princeton: Princeton University Press, 2001). Susan Bayly adopts a middle position between Dumont and Cohn and asserts that while caste is not an Oriental fiction, British colonial rule helped cement its place in the Indian context. See her *Caste, Society and Politics in India from the Eighteenth Century to the Modern Age* (Cambridge: Cambridge University Press, 1999).

19 Dumont, *Homo Hierarchicus*, 130.

20 He cites, for example, work done by Emile Senart, Edward Blunt, John Henry Hutton, and Henry Noel Stevenson.

21 Dumont, *Homo Hierarchicus*, 139.

22 Tissa Balasuriya has shown that not only social divisions, but also missiological presumptions, affect how people understand and celebrate a communal meal event like the Lord's Supper. He does this in reference to life in the Catholic Church in Sri Lanka during successive periods under Portuguese, Dutch, and British rule and since independence in 1948. See his *The Eucharist and Human Liberation* (Maryknoll, N.Y.: Orbis Books, 1979), 95–115.

23 This essay originally appeared in *Social Research* 66, no. 1 (Spring 1999), 133–149. It was republished in *Essays in Cultural Transmission* (New York: Berg, 2005), 45–59.
24 Bloch, *Essays in Cultural Transmission*, 45.
25 Ibid., 49.
26 Ibid., 57.
27 Cf. Audrey Hayley's claims regarding the meaning of certain offerings presented in worship by Assamese Hindus in his essay, "A Commensal Relationship with God: The nature of the offering in Assamese Vaishnavism" in *Sacrifice*, eds. M. F. C. Bourdillon and Meyer Fortes (London: Academic Press, 1980), 107–126.
28 *Food and Identity in Early Rabbinical Judaism* (Cambridge: Cambridge University Press, 2010), 185.
29 See, for example, Nathan MacDonald, *Not Bread Alone: The Uses of Food in the Old Testament* (Oxford: Oxford University Press, 2008); Jean Soler, "The Dietary Prohibitions of the Hebrews," *New York Review of Books*. June 14, 1979: 24–30. In a PhD dissertation submitted in 1995 at the Jewish Theological Seminary of America and entitled *The Literary Function of Eating and Drinking in Hebrew Bible Narrative with Reference to the Literatures of the Ancient Near East*, Diane Sharon illustrates how texts describing eating and drinking in the Hebrew Bible frequently exhibit a literary pattern of eating and drinking followed by an oracle.
30 Isidore Epstein, *Judaism: A Historical Presentation* (New York: Penguin Books, 1959), 26. Cf. David Freidenreich, *Foreigners and Their Food: Constructing Otherness in Jewish, Christian, and Islamic Law* (Berkeley: University of California Press 2011), 17–18.
31 George Foot Moore, *Judaism in the First Centuries of the Christian Era: The Age of the Tannaim*, Vol. II (Cambridge: Harvard University Press, 1954), 40–54.
32 Peter Altmann, *Festive Meals in Ancient Israel: Deuteronomy's Identity Politics in Their Ancient Near Eastern Context* (Berlin; New York: De Gruyter, 2011).
33 Altmann, *Festive Meals*, 294. It is noteworthy that, in the case of early rabbinical Judaism, restrictions on commensality were designed to form a distinct identity for groups. In *Food and Identity in Early Rabbinic Judaism* (Cambridge: Cambridge University Press, 2010), Jordan Rosenblum has argued that regulations affecting the use of food and dining practices helped construct the identity of early rabbinical Judaism. The Tannaim, he argues, "innovate and manipulate food practices to construct a distinctly Jewish, male, and rabbinic identity" (p. 186) and accomplished this through "regulating culinary and commensal practices" (p. 2).
34 Andrew McGowan has pointed to the danger of using scholarship about Jesus and the Gospels, rather than the community that succeeded him, as a source on which to predicate pastoral and liturgical practice. He helpfully clarifies, however, that it is possible to draw upon the sources

reflecting on the traditions of the historical Jesus to arrive at results that are shared by liturgical theologians who ground the doctrine and practice of the Eucharist rather in constructive theology than in historical research. See his essay "The Meals of Jesus and the Meals of the Church: Eucharistic Origins and Admission to Communion," *Studia Liturgica Diversa: Studies in Church Music and Liturgy—Essays in Honor of Paul F. Bradshaw*, eds. Maxwell Johnson and L. Edward Phillips (Portland, Oregon: Pastoral Press, 2004), 101–115.

35 On meals in the world in the ancient Near East and in the Greek and Roman traditions, see, for example, *Dining in a Classical Context*, ed. William J. Slater (Ann Arbor, Mich.: University of Michigan Press, 1991). See also Jerome Neyrey, "Meals, Food and Table Fellowship," *The Social Sciences and New Testament Interpretation*, ed. Richard L. Rohrbaugh (Peabody, Mass.: Hendrickson Publishers, 1996), 159–82.

36 Oswyn Murray, "Sympotic History" in *Sympotica: A Symposium on the Symposium*, ed. Oswyn Murray (Oxford: Clarendon Press, 1991), 5. Cf. Don R. Brothwell, "Foodstuffs, Cooking, and Drugs," in *Civilization of the Ancient Mediterranean, Greece and Rome* (New York: Charles Scribner's Sons, 1988), 1.247–61.

37 It would be profitable to reflect on the Lord's Supper and its relation to the meals of Jesus before and after his resurrection since these meal events contain a proclamation and enactment of the nearness of the rule of God.

38 Dennis Smith, *From Symposium to Eucharist: The Banquet in the Early Christian World* (Minneapolis: Fortress Press, 2003). In her review of this book, Andrea Lieber rightly emphasizes the importance of not ignoring or downplaying the ancient Israelite antecedents of the Lord's Supper by subsuming the variety of meals in the Greco-Roman world into a single category. See her review in *The Jewish Quarterly Review*, 96, no. 2 (Spring 2006), 263–267.

39 Dennis Smith, *From Symposium to Eucharist*, 9.

40 Ibid., 10.

41 Ibid., 10–11. Not surprisingly, the Lord's Supper came to be understood as a proper occasion when an offering could be collected in order that the community might help care for the financially dispossessed who were a part of their community. As Justin Martyr said in his *First Apology*, the president at the Eucharist should use the collection received "to help the orphans and widows and all who for any reason are in distress, whether because they are sick, in prison, or away from home. In a word, he takes care of all who are in need." See Justin's *The First Apology*, chapter 67.

42 Dennis Smith, "The Historical Jesus at Table," *Society of Biblical Literature 1989 Seminar Papers* (Atlanta, Ga.: Scholars Press, 1989), 469.

43 *More Than a Passover: Inculturation in the Supper Narratives of the New Testament* (Frankfurt am Main: Peter Lang, 2007).

44 King, *More Than a Passover*, 230.

45 Ibid., 231.
46 See note 52.
47 Gillian Feeley-Harnik, *The Lord's Table: Eucharist and Passover in Early Christianity* (Philadelphia: University of Pennsylvania Press, 1982), 2.
48 Feeley-Harnik, *The Lord's Table*, 19.
49 Ibid., 85 ff.
50 Ibid., 86.
51 Ibid., 86. She notes: "A person who shares fellowship with another 'enjoys his salt' (Ezekiel 4:14). A particularly intimate covenant is therefore called a 'covenant of salt' (Numbers 18:19; 2 Chronicles 13:5; Ezra 4:14). . . . Jesus says to his disciples, 'Have salt in yourselves, and be at peace with one another' (Mark 9:50; see also Matthew 5:13; Luke 14:34–35; Colossians 4:6)."
52 *Rediscovering the Lord's Supper: Communion with Israel, with Christ, and Among the Guests* (Atlanta, Ga.: John Knox Press, 1988), 71.
53 On Jesus' meals in the New Testament see, for example, Robert Karris, *Luke: Artist and Theologian* (New York: Paulist Press, 1985), especially 47–78; Dennis Smith, "The Historical Jesus at Table," *Society of Biblical Literature 1989 Seminar Papers* (Atlanta, Ga.: Scholars Press, 1989), 466–86; Jerome Neyrey, "Ceremonies in Luke-Acts: The Case of Meals and Table Fellowship" in his *The Social World of Luke–Acts. Models for Interpretation* (Peabody, Mass.: Hendrikson Publishers, 1991), 361–87; Scott Bartchy, "Table Fellowship" in *Dictionary of Jesus and the Gospels*, eds. Joel Green and Scot McKnight (Downers Grove, Ill.: InterVarsity Press, 1992), 796–800; and John Mark Hicks, *Come to the Table: Revisioning the Lord's Supper* (Abilene, Texas: Leafwood Publishers, 2002), especially 51–100.
54 "Baptism and the Lord's Supper as Community Acts: Toward a Sacramental Understanding of the Ordinances" in *Baptist Sacramentalism*, eds. Anthony Cross and Philip Thompson (Eugene, Oreg.: Wipf & Stock Publishers, 2003), 91.
55 See, for example, Geoffrey Wainwright, *Eucharist and Eschatology* (London: Epworth, 1971). Wainwright describes the eschatological content and features of the Eucharist whose connection with the Messianic feast he underlines in order to emphasize the dimensions of "the already" and "the not yet" of the eucharistic meal.
56 On the impact on New Testament texts of ideas of an eschatological meal and scenes of nutritional abundance in the Ancient Near East and the Mediterranean world, see Peter-Ben Smit, *Fellowship and Food in the Kingdom: Eschatological Meals and Scenes of Utopian Abundance in the New Testament* (Tübingen: Mohr Seibeck, 2008).
57 Norman Wirzba, *Food and Faith: A Theology of Eating* (Cambridge; Cambridge University Press, 2011), 234.
58 The anamnesis is not simply a mental recollection of Christ and his death. Nor is it an act to repeat what was done once and for all at Calvary. On the meaning of anamnesis, see *Baptism, Eucharist and Ministry* (Geneva:

World Council of Churches, 1982) § B 5–9. See also *Baptism, Eucharist and Ministry 1982–1990: Report on the Process and Responses* (Geneva: WC Publications, 1990), 62–63, 114–116. As anamnesis, Holy Communion is our remembering in celebration; it is more than recalling of past event. It is a representation, a reenactment without a repetition. It is a sacrifice of praise that makes present the eternal dimensions of Christ's sacrifice at Calvary. See Ernest Falardeau, *A Holy and Living Sacrifice: The Eucharist in Christian Perspective* (Collegeville, Minn.: The Liturgical Press, 1996), 24–33.

59 The discernment of the presence of the risen Christ becomes clear when the notion of the Lord's Supper as "sacrifice" is properly understood. See, for example, *Lutherans and Catholics in Dialogue 3: The Eucharist as Sacrifice* (New York: U.S.A. National Committee of the Lutheran World Federation and the Bishops' Committee for Ecumenical and interreligious Affairs, 1968). See also *Sacrifice and Modern Thought*, eds. Julia Meszaros and Johannes Zachhuber (Oxford: Oxford University Press, 2013).

60 *Baptism, Eucharist and Ministry 1982–1990*, 62.

61 Jean-Jacques von Allmen, *The Lord's Supper*, 55.

62 *The Orthodox Creed*, Article XIX, in *Baptist Confessions of Faith*, Second Revised Edition, edited by William Lumpkin and revised by Bill Leonard (Valley Forge, Pa.: Judson Press, 2011), 318. The text of the 1678 Orthodox Creed was influenced by both the Westminster Confession and the 1677 Second London Confession.

63 *The Orthodox Creed*, Article XXXIII, in *Baptist Confessions of Faith*, Second Revised Edition, 330–331.

64 1 Corinthians 10:16.

65 § E 19.

66 See R. Stephen Warner, "Religion, Boundaries, and Bridges," *Sociology of Religion* 58, no. 3 (Fall 1997), 217–238. On how the standing of women was affirmed in meal settings, see Kathleen Corley, *Private Women, Public Meals: Social Conflict in the Synoptic Tradition* (Peabody, Mass.: Hendrickson Publishers, 1993), especially chapter 2. See also Marcus Borg's explanation of how Jesus' "open commensality" with "sinners" challenged Jewish purity laws in his *Meeting Jesus Again for the First Time* (San Francisco: Harper, 1994), p. 56. See also Craig Blomberg, *Contagious Holiness: Jesus' Meals with Sinners* (Downers Grove, Ill.: InterVarsity Press, 2005).

67 For an assessment of the impact of *BEM* after twenty-five years, see *BEM at 25: Critical Insights into a Continuing Legacy*, eds. Thomas Best and Tamara Grdzelidze (Geneva: WCC Publications, 2007).

68 See, for example, the story of First Baptist Church in Richmond, Virginia. Whites and blacks had worshipped together at the church. In 1838, the minister, Jeremiah Jeter, argued that "neither group in the church would achieve its maximum effectiveness" with its "biracial membership." He opined that "the wisest way" to solve the "problem" was "to

bring about a separate house of worship and church organization for the Black Baptists in Richmond." So Jeter asked the church membership to "consider whether its white members might build in another place a house of worship for themselves, thus releasing for the use of the colored people their property at College and Broad streets. The proposal was accepted by members attending a meeting in which "the sisters and black members were not asked to participate." See Blanche White and Frederick Anderson, *The Open Door: A History of the First Baptist Church, Richmond, Virginia, 1780–2005* (Richmond, Va.: First Baptist Church, 2006), 57–59.

69 The published account of an attempt at an "interracial church merger" in South Carolina is highly instructive. See Kersten Priest and Robert Priest, "Divergent Worship Practices in the Sunday Morning Hour: Analysis of an 'Interracial' Church Merger" in *This Side of Heaven: Race, Ethnicity, and Christian Faith*, eds. Robert Priest and Alvaro Nieves (Oxford University Press, 2007), 275–291. Literature addressing the function of commensality in the African American Church tradition include Jualynne Dodson and Cheryl Gilkes, "There Is Nothing Like Church Food—Food and the US Afro-Christian Tradition: Remembering Community and Feeding the Embodied S/spirit(s)," *Journal of the American Academy of Religion*, 63, (1995), 519–538; and Frances Kostarelos, *Feeling the Spirit: Faith and Hope in an Evangelical Black Storefront Church* (Columbia: University of South Carolina Press, 1995). See Philip Perlmutter, *Divided We Fall: History of Ethnic, Religious and Racial Prejudice in America* (Ames, Iowa: Iowa State University Press, 1992), especially 53–108. "Contrary to contemporary sermonizing" Perlmutter says on page 107, "the closer some [ethnic] groups came to each other, the greater was their mutual distrust."

70 T. B. Maston, *Segregation and Desegregation: A Christian Approach* (New York: The Macmillan Company, 1959), 136.

71 According to some ecclesial traditions, the reference to "common baptism" is better expressed as "one baptism" mentioned in Ephesians 4:5. See, for example, Faith and Unity Executive Committee of the Baptist Union of Great Britain and The Council for Christian Unity of the Church of England, *Pushing at the Boundaries of Unity: Anglicans and Baptists in Conversation* (London: Church House Publishing, 2005), 31–57.

72 On the way the church responded to this awareness, see Werner Elert, *Eucharist and Church Fellowship in the First Four Centuries* trans. N. E. Nagel (St. Louis, Mo.: Concordia Publishing House, 1966).

73 Pilgram Marpek cited by John Rempel, *The Lord's Supper in Anabaptism: A Study of the Christology of Balthasar Hubmaier, Pilgram Marpek, and Dirk Philips* (Waterloo, Ontario: Herald Press, 1993), 129.

74 The Eucharist is not included in the Gospel of John. Gutierrez claims that John "substitutes the episode of the washing of the disciples' feet—a gesture of service, love, and brotherhood." *A Theology of Liberation*, trans.

and eds. Sister Caridad Indad and John Eagleson (Maryknoll, N.Y.: Orbis Books, 1973), 263.
75 Article 16. This 1611Confession is available in *Baptist Confessions of Faith*, Second Revised Edition, 112. Curtis Freeman's insistence on the Eucharist being regarded as "an act of common prayer" instead of "a matter of private devotion" highlights his convincing argument for a retrieval of the reality of the presence of the risen Christ through the Holy Spirit in the gathered community. See his *Contesting Catholicity*, 311–338.
76 Angel F. Mendez Montoya, *The Theology of Food: Eating and the Eucharist* (Chichester: Wiley-Blackwell, 2009), 114. On pages 113–156, Montoya develops "alimentary theology" as he explores the "theopolitical dimension of alimentation."
77 *Your Kingdom Come—Mission Perspectives: Report on the World Conference on Mission and Evangelism, Melbourne, Australia, 12–25 May 1980* (Geneva: World Council of Churches, 1980).
78 Ibid., 204.
79 Ibid., 205.
80 Ibid., 206.
81 Cf. Ephesians 1:10.
82 See *The Nature and Purpose of the Church: A Stage on the Way to a Common Statement*, Faith and Order Paper No. 181 (Geneva: WCC, 1998), §26–34. Cf. *The Nature and Mission of the Church*. Faith and Order Paper No. 198 (Geneva: World Council of Church, 2005), §34–42.
83 The literature on this subject is immense. It includes accessible and contemporary books such as Margaret Scott's *The Eucharist and Social Justice* (New York: Paulist Press, 2009), which is written with a global perspective. See also "Justice and the Eucharist" in *Living Bread, Saving Cup*, ed. R. Kevin Seasoltz (Collegeville, Minn.: The Liturgical Press, 1987) 305–323. In "Eucharistic Justice" *Theological Studies* 67:4 (December 2006): 856–879, David Power probes the connection between the Eucharist and the church's mission to promote justice.
84 1 Corinthians 11:18–22, NRSV.
85 Acts 4:32–35, NRSV.
86 For Susan Holman's overview of *leitougia* and the poor in the first six centuries CE, see especially *The Hungry Are Dying: Beggars and Bishops in Roman Cappadocia* (Oxford: Oxford University Press, 2001), 49–63.
87 *The Didache*, 14, 1–3 in *Early Church Fathers*, trans. and ed. Cyril Richardson (New York: Macmillan Publishing Co., Inc., 1970).
88 *The Didache*, chap. 9.
89 *The Didache* 14, 1–3. Divergent interpretations of this passage reflect different theories concerning the origins of the text. See, for example, Dennis Joseph Billy, *The Beauty of the Eucharist: Voices from the Church Fathers* (Hyde Park, N.Y.: New City Press, 2010), 47–56.
90 *Didascalia Apostolorum*, Chapter IX.ii.26 in Alistair Stewart-Sykes, *The Didascalia Apostolorum: An English Version with Introduction*

and Annotation (Turnhout, Belgium: Brepols Publishers, 2009), 151. Cf. what chapter XVII.iv.3 says in reference to Christian obligation. It declares that "anyone who has possessions and does not use himself, nor helps others, is laying up perishable treasure for himself on earth. He is in the position of the snake lying upon the treasure and is in danger of being reckoned alongside it." Ibid., 197.

91 *Epistle to the Ephesians*, chap. 5 and *Epistle to the Smyrnaeans*, chap. 4; *Early Christian Fathers*, edited by Cyril Richardson (New York: Macmillan & Co., 1970), 89; 113–114.
92 *Epistle to the Philadelphians*, chap. 4 in *Early Christian Fathers*, 108–109.
93 *Epistle to the Smyrnaeans*, chap. 6 and 7 in *Early Church Fathers*, 114.
94 *Epistle to the Polycarp*, chap. 4 in *Early Christian Fathers*, 119.
95 *The First Apology*, chap. 67, *Ante-Nicene Fathers*, Volume 1, eds. Alexander Roberts and James Donaldson (Peabody, Mass.: Hendrickson Publishers, 2004), 186. There is an echo of Justin's statement in the *Didascalia* 43, which came from the second or third century: "Therefore as good stewards of God, do well in dispensing the things that are given and come into the Church, according to the commandment, to the orphans and widows and those who are in straits and to strangers, like men who know that ye have a God who requires at your hands an account of the stewardship which He has committed to you. Therefore distribute and give to every one who is in want, also yourselves provide and live from these things, from the things that come into the Church. Do not consume them yourselves alone, but give a share with yourselves to those who are in want."
96 *First Apology*, XIV. *Ante-Nicene Fathers*, Volume 1, eds. Alexander Roberts and James Donaldson (Peabody, Mass.: Hendrickson Publishers, 2004), 167. For a general overview of the teaching of the early fathers on the subject of human solidarity, see Igino Giordani, *The Social Message of the Early Church Fathers*, 1944 (Boston: Daughters of St. Paul, 1977), 298–320.
97 Dennis Joseph Billy, *The Beauty of the Eucharist: Voices from the Church Fathers* (Hyde Park, N.Y.: New City Press, 2010), 65.
98 *Christ the Educator* 2.2.20 cited in *The Beauty of the Eucharist*, 80.
99 See André Méhat, "Clement of Alexandria" in *The Eucharist of the Early Christians*, Willy Rordorf and Others, trans. Matthew O'Connell (Collegeville, Minn.: The Liturgical Press, 1990), 107.
100 *The Stromata, or Miscellanies*, Bk. 2, chap. 9 in *Ante-Nicene Fathers*, Volume 2, edited by Alexander Roberts and James Donaldson (Peabody, Mass.: Hendrickson Publishers, 2004), 357.
101 *Epistle 62*, no. 13.
102 See *Treatise* 8:15 from his *On Works and Almsgiving*, available at www.ccel.org/ccel/schaff/anf05.iv.v.viii.html.
103 *Ante-Nicene Fathers*, Vol. 5, eds. Alexander Roberts and James Donaldson (Peabody, Mass.: Hendrickson Publishers, 2004), 314.

104 For an analysis of the Cappadocians' sermons on the poor, see Susan Holman, *The Hungry Are Dying*, especially chapters 3 and 4.
105 See David Rylaarsdam, *John Chrysostom on Divine Pedagogy: The Coherence of His Theology and Preaching* (Oxford: Oxford University Press, 2014), 145–146. The references to Chrysostom's works are copiously cited.
106 See John Chrysostom, *Homily XLVII: John vi. 53, 54. Nicene and Post-Nicene Fathers*, Volume 14, First Series, ed. Philip Schaff (Peabody, Mass.: Hendrickson Publishers, 2004), 172. Besides his many sermons on the care of the poor, John also promoted efforts to relieve the plight of the vulnerable. A concise description of John's philanthropic efforts is available in Wendy Mayer and Pauline Allen, *John Chrysostom* (London and New York: Routledge, 2000), 47–52.
107 *Homily on the Epistle to the Hebrews*, 10. 8. *Nicene and Post-Nicene Fathers*, Volume 14, First Series, ed. Philip Schaff (Peabody, Mass.: Hendrickson Publishers, 2004), 417. One wonders what influence Chrysostom's claim in his *Homily on Hebrews 10.8* might have had on Thomas Helwys' advocacy for proper regard for people's freedom of conscience, whether they be "heretics, Turks, Jews or whatsoever."
108 David Rylaarsdam, *John Chrysostom on Divine Pedagogy*, 147–148.
109 Ibid., 151.
110 The text of his sermons "To the Rich," "I Will Tear Down My Barns," "In Time of Famine and Drought," and "Against Those Who Lend at Interest" appear with a helpful introduction in *On Social Justice—St. Basil the Great*, Translation with Introduction and Commentary by C. Paul Schroeder (Crestwood, N.Y.: St Vladimir's Seminary Press, 2009). In the Introduction, Schroeder offers a synthesis of Basil's thought. He refers to the frequency of Basil's use of the adjective *koinos* to show Basil's disapproval of those who live on the basis of competition and to reveal Basil's commitment to the common sharing by all in the fruit of creation (see especially 31ff.). Schroeder also describes the community Basil founded to give expression to his social concern. This community, which later became known as *Basiliad*, was "a place where the poor and diseased were able to receive food, shelter, and medical treatment free of charge" (p. 33).
111 "To the Rich," 4 in *On Social Justice—St. Basil the Great*, 47.
112 Sermon on Luke 12:16–21, chap. 3, entitled "I Will Tear Down My Barns." See also chapters 6 and 7. In addition, the text of the Divine Liturgy in which Basil reinforces concern for the poor: "Remember, O Lord, those who bring offerings and do good in Thy holy churches, and those who remember the poor; reward them with your rich and heavenly gifts." He prays: "Defend the widows; protect the orphans; free the captives; heal the sick. Remember, O Lord, those who are in mines, in exile, in harsh labor, and those in any kind of affliction, necessity, or distress." The authorship of the Divine Liturgy of St. Basil is disputed, but it is possible that Basil himself supplied the core of the Anaphora.

113 Orations 8.18 cited in *The Beauty of the Eucharist*, 183.
114 Orations 45.19 cited in *The Beauty of the Eucharist*, 184.
115 Drawing from Gregory's *Catechetical Oration*, Hans Boersma shows how the author expounds the transformation made possible through the Eucharist. See *Embodiment and Virtue in Gregory of Nyssa: An Anagogical Approach* (Oxford: Oxford University Press, 2013), 186–188.
116 Gregory's sermon *On the Love of the Poor* is analyzed by Andrew Hofer, *Christ in the Life and Teaching of Gregory of Nazianzus* (Oxford: Oxford University Press, 2013), 222.
117 For discussions of Gregory's concern for the poor, see ibid., 220–224. See also Susan Holman, *The Hungry Are Dying*, 169–177.
118 Not surprisingly, he emphasized the sacrificial dimension of the Eucharist. He was convinced that "through the Eucharist the body comes into intimate union with its savior. . . . In the Eucharist, [Christ] unites our bodies with himself, so that mankind too, by its union with what is immortal, may share in incorruptibility." See his *Great Catechetical Oration*, chap. 37, cited in Anthony Meredith, *The Cappadocians* (London: Geoffrey Chapman, 1995), 96.
119 *Great Catechetical Oration*, chap. 37, cited in *The Beauty of the Eucharist*, 197–198.
120 Not to be forgotten is also Macrina, the sister of Basil of Caesarea and Gregory of Nyssa, who did the same through her example of "empathic relief." Finding people starving at the side of a road, she took them to her monastery and took care of them. (See Susan Holman, *God Knows There's Need*, 47–70. In chapter 3 of this book Holman paints a brilliant portrait of multiple ways in which the church in its earliest centuries exercised care for vulnerable people.)
121 Khalid Dinno, "Jacob of Serugh, The Man Behind the Mimre" in *Jacob of Serugh and His Times: Studies in Sixth-Century Syriac Christianity*, ed. George Anton Kiraz (Piscataway, N.Y.: Georgias Press, 2010), 51.
122 *Homily on the Reception of the Holy Mysteries*, cited by Amir Harrak, "The Syriac Orthodox Celebration of the Eucharist in Light of Jacob of Serugh's Mimrō 95" in *Jacob of Serugh and His Times*, 94 and 92. For an analysis of Mar Jacob's understanding of the Eucharist, see Hugh Connolly, *Jacob of Serugh on the Eucharist: Homilies 22 and 95* (Piscataway, N.J.: Gorgias Press, 2010).
123 From *On the Love of the Poor*, cited in Holman, 49–50.
124 In *Bread of Life and Cup of Joy*, 194–200, Horton Davies includes among those in the Western World who provided "glimpses of the social implications of the Eucharist"—"Christian socialists" like Frederick Maurice; Tractarians such as John Newman and Edward Pusey, Anglo-Catholics like Frank Weston, French worker-priests, and exponents in North America of the "Social Gospel." He also includes theologians such as Johann Baptist Metz, Jurgen Moltmann, Jean-Marie Tillard, and Nicholas Lash. However, many others from the seventh to the nineteenth century could also be cited.

125 *A Theology of Liberation*, 262–265.
126 Ibid., 263. For a seminal essay on covenant from a Baptist perspective, see Paul Fiddes, "'Walking Together': The Place of Covenant Theology in Baptist Life Yesterday and Today" in *Pilgrim Pathways: Essays in Baptist History in Honour of B. R. White*, eds. William Brackney and Paul Fiddes with John Briggs (Macon, Ga.: Mercer University Press, 1999), 47–74.
127 *A Theology of Liberation*, 265. Gutierrez read the story of the Spanish colonization and oppression of the people of the Indies in the light of his eucharistic hermeneutic. So, in evaluating the work in Hispaniola (Haiti and Dominican Republic) of the Spanish friar Antonio de Montesinos, Gutierrez noted Montesinos' understanding of the salvation Jesus proclaimed. It "must necessarily have repercussions on temporal history." So, Montesinos "sketched out a criticism of the economic, social, and religious causes of the oppression suffered by Indians." Gutiérrez emphasizes, however, that "to criticize their servitude, as well as the legal and Christian considerations being brought forward for its justification, was surely an important task. But it was also necessary, and urgent, to knock away the underpinnings of the specious justification of the social system then being established in the Indies." See Gustavo Gutiérrez, *Las Casas: In Search of the Poor of Jesus Christ*, trans. Robert Barr (Maryknoll, N.Y.: Orbis Books, 1993), 35, 37–38.
128 *The Eucharist and Human Liberation*, 3. Balasuriya issues a lament: "The Eucharist has been domesticated within the dominant social establishments of the day. Its radical demands have been largely neutralized. Its cutting edge has been blunted. Worse still it has been and is still being used as legitimation of cruel exploitation." See ibid., 2.
129 Ibid., 17.
130 Ibid., 22.
131 Ibid., 142.
132 Ibid., especially 23–58 and 128–145.
133 *Gathering for Worship: Patterns and Prayers for the Community of Disciples*, eds. Christopher Ellis and Myra Blythe for the Baptist Union of Great Britain (Norwich: Canterbury Press, 2005), 35.
134 Especially in traditions that affirm transubstantiation and, as in the mystery cults in the Greco-Roman world, teach that communicants eat the flesh and drink the blood of Christ, and so affirm the common source of their life and their common participation in the life of the one they worship, the segregation of communicants into ethnic camps is particularly noteworthy. See, for example, Stephen Harris, *Understanding the Bible*, Mayfield Publishing Co. 8th ed. (McGraw-Hill Publishing, 2010), 286–7.
135 von Allmen, *The Lord's Supper*, 59.
136 As Randy Hohf has explained, Holy Communion is not merely a fellowship meal. It is also a covenant meal. See his *Biblical Perspectives on Fellowship Meals* available at www.bogadocious.com/meat/LS.pdf.

136 NOTES

137 T. B. Maston, *Segregation and Desegregation* (New York: The Macmillan Company, 1959), 133.
138 *Nature and Mission of the Church* §81. On this see, Eduardus Van der Borght, "No Longer Strangers in the Church? Socio-cultural Identities in the Faith and Order Document *Nature and Mission of the Church*" in *Strangers and Pilgrims on Earth: Essays in Honour of Abraham Van de Beek*, eds. Eduardus Van der Borght and Paul Van Geest (Leiden & Boston: Brill, 2013), 431–444.
139 Gutierrez, *A Theology of Liberation*, 267.

Chapter 4

1 Kortright Davis, *Serving with Power: Reviving the Spirit of Christian Ministry* (Mahwah, N.J.: Paulist Press, 1999), 172.
2 Edmund Davis, *Courage and Commitment* (Mona, Kingston: University of the West Indies Publishers Association, 1988), 51.
3 Adolfo Ham, "Caribbean Theology: The Challenge of the Twenty-First Century" in *Caribbean Theology: Preparing for the Challenges Ahead*, ed. Howard Gregory (Mona, Kingston: Canoe Press, 1995), 4.
4 *Minutes of the Meeting of the Faith and Order Standing Commission 5—12 January 1995, Aleppo, Syria*, Faith and Order Paper No. 170, (Geneva: World Council of Churches, 1995), 105–106.
5 In this perspective, it is entirely legitimate that many representations of the Christmas crèche exist, and these reflect admirably the cultural context of those creating the art form depicting the birth of the Christ child.
6 *Participating in God's Mission of Reconciliation*, §127.
7 The classical discussion of the relationship between Christ and civilization is found in H. Richard Niebuhr's *Christ and Culture* (New York: Harper & Row, Publishers, 1951).
8 See especially William Watty, *From Shore to Shore: Soundings in Caribbean Theology* (Kingston, Jamaica, 1981), 51–61.
9 See, for example, Sallie McFague, *The Body of God: An Ecological Theology* (Minneapolis: Augsburg Fortress, 1993) and Grace Jantzen, *God's World, God's Body* (Philadelphia: Westminster John Knox Press, 1984).
10 See *Incarnation: On the Scope and Depth of Christology*, ed. Niels Gregersen (Minneapolis: Fortress Publishers, 2015).
11 See especially, Elizabeth Jonson, "Jesus and the Cosmos: Soundings in Deep Christology" in ibid., 133–156.
12 Garnet Roper, *Caribbean Theology as Public Theology* (Kingston: Xpress Litho, 2012), 170. Any reading of Caribbean history that ignores the development of Caribbean theology is likely to misconstrue the role of religion in Caribbean development and present a caricature that is similar to the one preserved by Patrick Hylton in *The Role of Religion in Caribbean History: From Amerindian Shamanism to Rastafarianism*

(Washington, D.C.: Billpops Publications, 2002). Compare Hylton's account with the one appearing in *Christianity in the Caribbean: Essays on Church History*, ed. Armando Lampe (Mona, Kingtson: The University of the West Indies Press, 2001).
13 Foreword to *Troubling the Waters* (San Fernando: Rahman Printery Ltd., 1973), 4.
14 Ibid., 5.
15 "What Will a Caribbean Christ Look Like? A Preface to Caribbean Christology" in *Out of the Depths*, ed. Idris Hamid (Trinidad: St Andrew's Theological College, 1977), 1.
16 *In Search of New Perspectives* (Barbados: Caribbean Ecumenical Consultation for Development, 1971), 8.
17 Ibid., 23–24. See also Idris Hamid, "Theology and Caribbean Development" in *With Eyes Wide Open*, ed. David Mitchell (Bridgetown: Christian Action for Development in the Caribbean—CADEC, 1973), 120–133. Cf. Idris Hamid, "Decolonizing the Christian Faith: A Fresh Approach to the Christian Faith in the Context of the Caribbean" in *Fambli: The Church's Responsibility to the Family in the Caribbean*, ed. Lilith Haynes (New York: Church World Service, c. 1972). 152–172.
18 (San Fernando, Trinidad: Rahman Printery Ltd., 1973).
19 "The De-Colonization of Theology" in *Troubling the Waters*, 75.
20 *From Shore to Shore*, 66.
21 Ibid., 65.
22 Ibid., 69.
23 Ibid., 60. In *Ministry at the Margins: Stories of Struggle, Survival and Transformation at the Margins of Society* (Kingston: Caribbean Graduate School of Theology, 2011), 230. Barry Wade states: "The incarnation of God . . . means God becoming real to men and women in the person and power of Jesus Christ and the Holy Spirit in every dimension of their lives."
24 Ibid., 61, cf. Lewin Williams, *Caribbean Theology* (New York: Peter Lang, 1994), especially 102–112.
25 See, for example, *Real Roots and Potted Plants: Reflections on the Caribbean Church* (Mandeville: Mandeville Publishers, 1984) and *Emerging from Innocence: Religion, Theology and Development* (Mandeville: Eureka Press, 1991).
26 Ashley Smith, *Real Roots*, 44–45.
27 Ibid., 45, 50. Roderick Hewitt regards the neglect of mission studies as central to the curriculum for ministerial training in the Caribbean as one aspect of the Eurocentric theological heritage of the Caribbean. See his "Christian Mission Studies in the Caribbean: Prospects and Challenges for the 21st Century" in *Development: Journal for Ministry and Mission* 1, no.1 (March 2004): 5–15.
28 Ashley Smith, "Mission and Evangelism in an Age of De-Colonisation" in *Out of the Depths*, 1977), 115–125.

29 Ashley Smith, *Emerging from Innocence*, 8.
30 Kortright Davis, *Mission for Caribbean Change: Caribbean Development as Theological Enterprise* (Frankfurt am Main, Bern: Verlag Peter Lang, 1982), 114.
31 Ibid., 134.
32 Ibid., 131.
33 Ibid., 135.
34 Ibid., 132.
35 Oral Thomas has shown that the motif of exodus is understood in various ways by Caribbean theologians. He also observes that, in some writings classified under Caribbean Theology, the theme of liberation rests not solely on the exodus, but also on the ancient Israelite prophetic tradition. Thomas' primary concern is to call participants in the Caribbean Theology movement to focus not only on the meaning of the biblical text for the existential reality of Caribbean people, but also on "the socio-ideological interests and social practices that have influenced the theological shape of the biblical text." See his *Biblical Resistance Hermeneutics within a Caribbean Context* (London: Equinox, 2010). In a welcome contribution to Caribbean Theology, Anna Perkins has shown the danger and limitation of reliance on Exodus imagery, interpreted "naively, selectively, and uncritically." She underscores the need to take seriously the ambiguity and plurality of narratives of the Exodus that include liberation, conquest, and displacement. See Anna Perkins, "Resisting Definitive Interpretation: Seeing the Story of the Exodus through Caribbean(ite) Eyes," *Caribbean Quarterly*, 51, no. 2 (June 2005), 53–66. In his essay, which has not gained its rightful place in the evolution of a hermeneutics for Caribbean Theology, Guyanese theologian Dale Bisnauth asserted: "A rediscovery of the historical and cultural milieu in which the Bible was 'produced' enables us to contextualize the biblical message." He emphasized, however, that "before the story of the Bible became God's word, it was God's event: We look for God's epiphany not in the text in the first place, but where God is acting savingly and in the lives and struggles of people." See his "Biblical Roots of Liberation Theology" in *Looking at the Theology of Liberation Together: An Ecumenical Reflection within the Caribbean*, ed. Burchell Taylor (Kingston: Jamaica Council of Churches, 1994), 1–20.
36 Kortright Davis, *Emancipation Still Comin': Explorations in Caribbean Emancipatory Theology* (Maryknoll, New York: Orbis, 1990), 50–55. Note Davis' concern for multiple expressions of faith in his focus on the church as "community of communities" in his book *Serving with Power: Reviving the Spirit of Christian Ministry* (New York: Paulist Press, 1999), 100–107. Interestingly, long before the category of the "nones" was created, Davis includes "Nowhereanism" in his list of religious affiliation in the region.
37 Lewin Williams, *Caribbean Theology*, 151. Williams offers what has come to be regarded as the standard text on the subject.

38 Ibid.
39 *Caribbean Theology*, 38–39.
40 See his essay "The Babylonish Captivity of the Church in the Caribbean" in *Caribbean Journal of Religious Studies (CJRS)* 4, no. 1 (April 1982), 1–16. Note that Taylor applies the liberation critique evident in that essay in two of his subsequent publications: *The Church Taking Sides* (Kingston: Bethel Baptist Church, 1995) and *Saying No to Babylon: A Reading of the Book of Daniel* (Kingston: Express Litho, 2006).
41 "The Babylonish Captivity," 2–3.
42 *Caribbean Theology as Public Theology*, 15.
43 Ibid.
44 Ibid., 174.
45 Ibid., 18.
46 Ibid., 170.
47 Idris Hamid, "Theology and Caribbean Development," 124. For a consideration of Christian ministry among the indigenous Caribbean people in the sixteenth-century Caribbean, see Noel Titus, *Conflicts and Contradictions: The Introduction of Christianity to the Sixteenth Century Caribbean* (London: Minerva Press, 1998). See especially 134–172. Cf. Mozella Mitchell, *Crucial Issues in Caribbean Religions* (New York: Peter Lang, 2006), especially 1–24.
48 Patrick Anthony, "A Case Study in Indigenization" in *Out of the Depths*, 1977, 192.
49 Kortright Davis *Emancipation Still Comin': Explorations in Caribbean Emancipatory Theology* (Maryknoll: Orbis, 1990), 90.
50 George Mulrain, *Theology in Folk Culture: The Theological Significance of Haitian Folk Religion* (Frankfurt am Main: Peter Lang, 1984), 369.
51 See ibid. and Carlton Dennis, *Proverbs and the People: A Comparative Study of Afro-Caribbean and Biblical Proverbs*. PhD Thesis, Drew University, 1995.
52 Michael St. A. Miller cites Sankeralli's articles that appeared in the Trinidadian newspaper, the *Sunday Express*. See Miller's *Reshaping the Contextual Vision in Caribbean Theology: Theoretical Foundations for Theology which Is Contextual, Pluralistic, and Dialectical* (Lanham: University Press of America, 2007), 13–14. See also Sankeralli's comments on the failure of what he calls "the creole paradigm" that seeks to articulate an authentic theology for the Caribbean region. See "Response to Dr. Lewin Williams' Paper, 'Invigorating the Caribbean Theological Enterprise: Learning from the Past, Forging a Path to the Future,'" *Caribbean Journal of Religious Studies (CJRS)*, 20:1 (1999), 31–34. For an interpretation of the struggle of Caribbean people to make room for the African heritage of the majority of the people by "resisting the dominating efforts of European colonizers and their descendants," see *The African-Caribbean Caribbean Worldview and the Making of Caribbean Society*, ed. Horace Levy (Kingston: The University of the West Indies Press, 2009).

53 *Troubling the Water*, ed. Idris Hamid (San Fernando: Rahman Printery, Ltd., 1973).
54 *Decolonising Theology: A Caribbean Perspective* (Maryknoll, N.Y.: Orbis, 1981), 97–115. Lewin Williams also criticizes Caribbean Theology for not paying adequate attention to consideration of gender. He laments "the absolutization of Christianity in settings where other religions exist and are practiced with comparable fervor." See his "Invigorating the Caribbean Theological Enterprise," *CJRS* 20, no. 1 (1999), 17–18; 20.
55 Michael Miller, *Reshaping the Contextual Vision in Caribbean Theology* and Livingston Thompson, *A Protestant Theology of Religious Pluralism* (Berne: Peter Lang, 2009). Meanwhile, Caribbean theologians have continued to agree on the need to incorporate within Caribbean Theology a discussion on the multiple Caribbean religious context instead of engaging in dialogue with Miller and Thompson. See two essays that appear in *Justice and Peace in a Renewed Caribbean: Contemporary Catholic Reflections*, Anna Kasafi Perkins, Donald Chambers, and Jacqueline Porter, eds. (New York: Palgrave Macmillan, 2012). One is by Anna Perkins, "Introduction: The Caribbean, Shaped by the Call for Justice and Peace," pp. 1–40, and the other by Gerald Boodoo, "Eucharist and Hospitality: Reflections on Stewardship and the Revitalization of Parish Life in the Caribbean," pp. 179–200. Perkins asks for other religions in the Caribbean to be treated "with the requisite seriousness." See especially pp. 18–22. Boodoo situates his call for discussion on interfaith relations and Caribbean identity within a dialogue on hospitality as a central aspect of stewardship. See pp. 190–193.
56 Michael Miller, *Reshaping the Contextual Vision in Caribbean Theology*, viii., x, and 28.
57 Ibid., 28.
58 Ibid., 214–216, 359, and 246.
59 Thompson, *A Protestant Theology*, 134–164; 191–240. Cf. Marie Reynolds, "Toward an Evangelical Caribbean Theology," *Binah* 1 (1996): 23–33. In her description of the contours Caribbean Theology, Reynolds emphasizes the need for its evangelical authenticity and asserts, as the litmus test of this, the theology subscribing to "biblical authority as the primary source of theology."
60 Livingston Thompson, *A Protestant Theology*, 21; 324–330.
61 Ibid., 319–324; 330–346.
62 Horace Russell, "The Challenge of Theological Reflection in the Caribbean Today" in *Troubling the Waters*, 25–34.
63 See the documents associated with the Faith and Order project, Ethnic Identity, National Identity and the Unity of the Church, such as *Participating in God's Mission*. See also *Church and World: The Unity of the Church and the Renewal of Human Community*, Faith and Order Paper No. 151 (Geneva: WCC Publications, 1990).
64 It is interesting to note how the construction of self-identity is influenced by the linkages between ethnicity, gender, and religion. See, for example,

Nicole Rodriguez Toulis, *Believing Identity: Pentecostalism and the Mediation of Jamaican Ethnicity and Gender in England* (Oxford and New York: Berg, 1997).
65 Theresa Lowe-Ching, "Method in Caribbean Theology" in *Caribbean Theology: Preparing for the Challenges Ahead*, ed. Howard Gregory (Kingston; Canoe Press, 1995), 23–33.
66 Althea Spencer Miller, "Women and Christianity in the Caribbean: Living Past the Colonial Legacy" in *Women and Christianity*, eds. Cheryl Kirk-Duggin and Karen Torjesen (Santa Barbara, Calif.: Praeger, 2010), 273–303.
67 Ibid., 273.
68 Ibid., 282.
69 Ibid., 292.
70 Hyacinth Boothe, "A Theological Journey for an Emancipatory Theology: Gospel and Culture," *CJRS* 17, no. 1 (April 1996), 15–21.
71 *Justice as Equality: Michael Manley's Caribbean Vision of Justice* (New York: Peter Lang, 2010).
72 Ibid., 6.
73 Ibid., 124.
74 Anna Perkins, "Resisting Definitive Interpretation: Seeing the Story of the Exodus through Caribbean(ite) Eyes," *Caribbean Quarterly* 51.2 (June 2005), 56.
75 See Anna Perkins, "Constructing an Egalitarian Society: Women, Social Ethics, and the Policy Imperatives of Michael Manley's 'Justice as Equality'" in *A Kairos Moment for Caribbean Theology: Ecumenical Voices in Dialogue*, Garnet Roper and J. Richard Middleton, eds. (Eugene, Ore.: Pickwick, 2013), 165–181.
76 Delores Williams, *Sisters in the Wilderness: The Challenge of Womanist God-Talk* (Maryknoll, N.Y.: Orbis Books, 1993).
77 Ibid., 61.
78 Ibid., 35.
79 The Gender and Development Studies (CGDS) traces its heritage to the global momentum for change created by the Women's Movement in the 1960s and 1970s. Its emergence was marked by the introduction of the Women and Development Unit at the UWI Cave Hill campus in the late 1970s. In 1992, the CGDS was established and in 2008, the UWI Council voted to upgrade the CGDS from a Centre to an Institute of the university. See http://www.mona.uwi.edu/igds/history.php. See also, Elsa Leo-Rhynie, "Women and Gender Studies: Moving from the Periphery" in Muhammed, *Gendered Realities*, 147–164.
80 Bridget Brereton, "Gendered Testimonies: Autobiographies, Diaries and Letters by Women as Sources for Caribbean History," *Feminist Review* 59 (Summer 1998), 143–163.
81 See Lucille Mathurin-Mair, *A Historical Study of Women in Jamaica 1655–1844*, eds. Hilary Beckles and Verene Shepherd (Kingston, Jamaica: Mona; University of the West Indies Press & Centre for Gender and Development Studies, 2006).

82 See, for example, *Engendering History: Caribbean Women in Historical Perspective*, eds. Verene Shepherd, Bridget Brereton, and Barbara Bailey (Kingston, Jamaica: Ian Randle Publishers, 1995); Hilary Beckles, *Centering Woman: Gender Discourses in Caribbean Slave Society* (Kingston, Jamaica: Ian Randle Publishers, 1999); *Women in Caribbean History: The British Colonised Territories*, ed. Verene Shepherd (Kingston, Jamaica: Ian Randle Publishers, 1999); Sandra Pouchet Paquet, *Caribbean Autobiography: Cultural Identity and Self-Representation* (Madison: University of Wisconsin Press, 2002); and David Williams, "Rereading Our Classics: In the Castle of My Skin and the Lonely Londoners," in *Gendered Realities*, 291–296.

83 In 1998, in an issue of a widely read journal dedicated to "Rethinking Caribbean Difference," Rawwida Baksh-Soodeen had criticized Caribbean feminism for its too-narrow Afrocentric focus. She took note, however, of the new wave of voices from the Indo-Caribbean. See her "Issues of Difference in Contemporary Caribbean Feminism" *Feminist Review* 59 (Summer, 1998): 74–85.

84 Rhoda Reddock, "The Indentureship Experience: Indian Women in Trinidad and Tobago, 1845–1917," in *Women Plantation Workers: International Experiences*, eds. Shobhita Jain and Rhoda Reddock (Kingston, Jamaica: University of the West Indies Press, 2004), 29. From as early as 1994, however, Verene Shepherd published her *Transients to Setters: The Experience of Indians in Jamaica, 1845–1950* (Leeds, England: Peepal Tree, University of Warwick, 1994). This was a revised version of the master's thesis that she had submitted at the University of the West Indies.

85 *Women Plantation Workers: International Experiences*, eds. Shobita Jain and Rhoda E. Reddock (London: Bloomsbury Academic, 1998), focuses on ways in which plantations in colonial outposts have impacted female population laborers over the last four centuries and highlights the efforts female workers made to resist their oppressive condition.

86 See, for example, Lucille Mathurin-Mair, "Women Field Workers in Jamaica During Slavery" in *Women Plantation Workers*, 17–27. The author analyzes "the pattern of sex-differentiated labour deployment" on the plantation and the struggle and resistance by enslaved women of African descent against the might of the plantation. She implicates the plantation system for reinforcing images of male control in the labor market.

87 Rhoda Reddock, "The Indentureship Experience: Indian Women in Trinidad and Tobago, 1845–1917" in *Women Plantation Workers*, 29–48. Reddock argues that the plantation's creation of a dichotomy between "light work" and "heavy work" was a strategy to devalue women's labor.

88 Verene A. Shepherd, "Indian Migrant Women and Plantation Labour in Nineteenth and Twentieth Century Jamaica: Gender Perspectives" in *Women Plantation Workers*, 89–106, claims that prevailing values

regarding men's place in the public domain and women's in their homes negatively impacted Indian women workers in Jamaica during and after indentureship. Shepherd argues that "research reveals that the experience of proletarianization and racial and ethnic oppression was not the same for men and women" in the history of plantation labor. She argues that Indian female laborers in Jamaica were subjected to "ultra-exploitability," and gender ideology contributed to this.

89 See, for example, Verene A. Shepherd, *Maharani's Misery: Narratives of a Passage from India to the Caribbean* (Kingston: University of the West Indies Press, 2002); Roseanne Kanhai, *Maticor: The Politics of Identity for Indo-Caribbean Women* (St Augustine: University of the West Indies School of Continuing Studies, 1999); Patricia Muhammed, *Gender Negotiations among Indians in Trinidad, 1917–1947* (New York: Pelgrave Macmillan, 2002); and Roseanne Kanhai, *Bindi: The Multifaceted Lives of Indo-Caribbean Women* (Mona, Kingston: University of the West Indies Press, 2011).

90 Elsa Leo-Rhynie, "Women and Gender Studies: Moving from the Periphery" in *Gendered Realities*, 147–164. Harold Sitahal, "Caribbean Theology of the people/for the People," in *CJRS* 20, no. 2 (1999), 3–17, has identified "participation, solidarity and collaboration with the 'people of God' in the region and also beyond" as a priority of the region. He calls for the involvement of the laity in the development of Caribbean Theology.

91 Faye Harrison, "Women in Jamaica's Urban Informal Economy: Insights from a Kingston Slum," in *Third World Women and the Politics of Feminism*, eds. Chandra Mohanty, Ann Russo and Lordes Torres (Bloomington: University of Indiana Press, 1991, 173–196).

92 See, for example, http://www.mona.uwi.edu/igds/publications.php, regarding Dunn report on *Trafficking and commercial sexual exploitation of children in Jamaica*, 2009, and her *Baseline Study of Household Workers in Jamaica for UN Women/Ministry of Labour Project Advancing Decent Work for Domestic Workers*, 2014.

93 Haleh Afsar, "Fluidities of Identities: Some Strategic and Practical Pathways Selected by Women," in *Women and Fluid Identities: Some Strategic and Practical Pathways Selected by Women*, ed. Haleh Afsar (New York: Palgrave Macmillan, 2012), 1, 7.

94 Gloria Joseph, "Caribbean Women: The Impact of Race, Sex, and Class" in *Comparative Perspectives of Third World Women: The Impact of Race, Sex, and Class*, ed. Beverley Lindsay (New York: Praeger Publishers, 1980), 143–161.

95 See, for example, Valerie Youssef, "Finding Self in the Transition from East to West: Indo-Trinidadian Perspectives" in *Bindi: The Multifaceted Lives*, chapter 4; and Patricia Muhammed, *Gender Negotiations Among Indians in Trinidad 1917–1947* (London: Palgrave Macmillan, 2002).

96 In his essay, Beckles argues that Afro-Caribbean masculinity emerged in the context of plantation life through the interaction between ruling

whites and enslaved blacks in which power was based on status, ownership of property (including human beings), and economic control. Black men came to share certain patriarchal values of the whites for whom they worked. This includes the assertion of masculine authority and power over women. Yet their humanity being denied and given their inability to put their vision into practice, blacks ended up with a subordinated masculinity, which they asserted when the opportunity arose. See Hilary Beckles, "Black Masculinity in Caribbean Slavery" in *Interrogating Caribbean Masculinities*: *Theoretical and Empirical Analyses*, ed. Rhoda Reddock (Kingston: University of the West Indies Press, 2004), 225–243. See also chapter one by Keith Nurse on "Theorizing Caribbean Masculinities: Masculinities in Transition—Gender and the Global Problematique." David William's essay was referenced in Note 133 and Linden Lewis contributed a chapter on "Masculinity and the Dance of the Dragon: Reading Lovelace Discursively" in *Feminist Review* 59 (Summer 1998): 164–185.

97 Ofelia Ortega, "God Has Called Us: Caribbean Women Searching for a Better Future," *CJRS* 20, no. 2 (1999), 38–49.

ABOUT THE AUTHOR

Neville George Callam, General Secretary of the Baptist World Alliance, was born in Jamaica. His training for the Christian ministry took him to the United Theological College of the West Indies, the University of the West Indies, and Harvard Divinity School. His wide range of interests and his commitment to community development have led him to serve in many capacities in both church and society. He has served as theological educator and media manager, pastor and church administrator. An ecumenist, he served on the Standing Commission on Faith and Order of the World Council of Churches from 1994 to 2007.

Ordained to the Christian ministry by the Jamaica Baptist Union (JBU) in 1977, his association with the Baptist World Alliance (BWA) began in 1985. He participated in the BWA as a member of the Executive Committee and General Council and served a five-year term as a BWA vice president.

Author or editor of seven books, including *Pursuing Unity and Defending Rights: The Baptist World Alliance at Work* (2010), Dr. Callam has made presentations at forums, seminars, workshops, and services of worship in more than eighty countries.